The Scent of Jasmine

by
Lioness DeWinter

ISBN #978-1-304-40718-4

For Anna Davis, and for my Mother

The Scent of Jasmine

Chapter One

It's a sultry night, hot and humid with a sunset like a fresh razor slash. The moon finally rises in the sky, heavy with the promise of blood and bursting with the sticky aura of forbidden sex. Evenings like this are the norm in New Orleans, where the voices of the past throb with the sacred drums of Santeria, and the echoes of old magic murmur feverishly under the stars and under the breath of the land.

It is in the air tonight, sharp and salty...strong enough to taste on my tongue. I am up for the games this night, circling and sniffing and Pavlovian in my lust. A monster of many disguises, a shape-shifter am I. My hair is as black as the heart of a Holocaust God; my eyes are the color of frozen rivers, and *fierce*, with a thick fringe of black lashes. It's been said that I'm a handsome man, and I have never had a reason to doubt it. I have had a great abundance of lovers, both male and female. They are drawn to my sharp, angular face, my tall stature, my broad shoulders and long limbs...and my large hands. A young lady from my past told me that my hands were beautiful, like the hands of Christ.

I hold my hands out in front of me, fingers outstretched, palms down. My hands, which have performed numerous tasks of extreme rapture, have also wrought much havoc in this world...

Hands of Christ.

Indeed.

I smile grimly.

Suddenly, I stop. My hands clench into fists as I flip back my hair and listen to the night. There is a psychic energy, a keening. I sniff the air a couple of times, and then head in the direction from where the scent emits the strongest.

Human fear and misery has a distinct scent, like freshly cut jasmine.

I breathe deeply, shivering with joy. My senses are honed like a thousand razor blades...

A park bench is where I find him, his head in his hands. His flowing, raven hair tumbles to the ground, as if ink from a bottle, as shining and straight as a slice of the night. He is dressed much as I, in black, watered silk, leather and lace, with platform boots of shining patent, and a long, leather coat cut in the style of 200 years past.

He doesn't notice me right away. I take him in for a moment, savoring the sight of this poor creature (obviously a prostitute), grateful that I will be the one to ease his pain--gently--and with finesse.

He raises his head and looks at me, and for a moment, I'm taken aback by his innocence. His large, brown eyes are shimmering with unshed tears, his mouth is full and soft, and his skin is alabaster white.

He looks so miserable, my heart aches for him. He is near my age (I'm guessing nineteen or twenty), and has the weight of the ages embedded in his soul, like a modern day Sisyphus.

I reach out with the fingertips of my psychic mind, and touch the mental wall of his. I lay my palm flat against it. It gives a bit. We are six feet apart, but he gives a small gasp, and his eyes widen.

He studies me warily, and I look calmly back at him. We study each other a long time...he seated, and I standing. There is fear in his eyes, and in his scent.

Jasmine.

He is afraid of me.

He *should* be.

I'm not offended by it.

I move closer, then reach out and touch his hair with the back of my hand. His eyes threaten to spill over with his misery. They glimmer and flash in the moonlight, then overflow onto the softness of his cheeks.

Mentally, I press my hand against the wall in his mind and push it back further. He gasps as if I've hurt him. My heart wrenches in sorrow (*why*?), as I press the palm of my hand against his hair and guide his head to my hip. He cries silently, my hands in his hair (was there *ever* such hair?), and he clasps his arms around my legs as if he's drowning.

On the street, people are staring. With contempt for the stupid sheep of humanity which I don't even bother trying to conceal, I encircle him with my arm, and cover him with my coat. They think that he is servicing me.

I scowl.

Fools.

Here in Orleans, they know my kind well, and they keep a respectful distance.

Now there are more pressing matters.

His tears have faded, and he is only sniffling a bit. I give him my handkerchief, an absurd old thing made of old lace, which only leaves his skin red and raw-looking under the streaks in his carefully made-up face.

Without a word, we move twenty feet over to the fountain, and I wet the handkerchief in the water and hold it to the swelling on his face. His eyes meet mine, and a hint of a smile plays at the corners of his lips.

I reach inside my coat and produce a bottle of wine and two glasses.

There is a sudden wisdom in his eyes, a knowing.

He sits pigeon-toed, sipping his wine, as I toy with the heavy lace ascot, and the obsidian pin at his throat.

He makes no move to help, and blushes quite appealingly.

I watch his face as I slowly unwrap the gauzy covering at his neck; he studies me though saucily lowered eyelashes.

I tuck a strand of his hair behind his ear, and reach out yet again with my mind to push back the mental wall of his inhibitions. It moves aside easily.

I open my mouth and press my lips against the side of his throat. He gasps; I pull his hair to one side and taste the nape of his neck, his hair like cashmere against my skin. I lick the back of his ear.

"You're so *pretty*," I groan.

I slip my hand into his shirt and run my fingertips over his chest. I can feel the nerve endings humming with life; I can smell the scorching hot blood beneath his skin.

He raises his face in ecstasy as my mouth once again finds the side of his throat. My fingers trail down his chest, over his smooth belly, and down to his trousers.

The pulse at his neck jumps violently; I kiss him there, my lips against his soft, white, alabaster throat...

He gasps. Pants.

I pull him back against me. He is fully alive in every sense of the word. He arches his back and throws his head back against me, as my lips once again find his pulse, so voluptuous and full of life. I press my lips down hard, part them, and feel his heartbeat against my tongue and my teeth.

He whimpers, as I emit a purring moan.

"Not *here*," he begs, his voice deep and thick as black velvet, and smoky with desire.

"Then *where?*" I murmur into his ear, my hands busy. He is firm in my hand, trembling. My other hand is cupping his breast from behind. His heartbeat is thundering against the palm of my hand, against my fingertips.

He is close to climax, panting, weakly protesting, as I beg him for his mouth. He snarls wordlessly.

I'm so hard, I ache.

He turns to me, panting.

"Let's go, it isn't far."

We walk together silently. He takes my arm with a shy smile when I offer it. His eyes are a warm, luminous brown, still heavily lined in black.

'*What a wondrous beauty he is,*' I think silently. '*Pity, really.*'

A troubled look appears very suddenly on his face, and he is looking at me in alarm. Then, just as quickly as the expression has come, it's gone.

I close my eyes with relief and sigh.

In a moment, I feel his breath on my face.

"Come," he whispers, "We're here."

Chapter Two

We are in an old house in the French Quarter. The room's walls are cherry red, with ebony trim. The pecan floor has been polished to a high sheen, and the high, oval windows are hung heavily with tapestries. Oriental rugs stretch across the vast expanse of the floor, and overstuffed, claw-footed furniture surrounds us. There is an old world charm about the place, mixed with the sensual gaudiness and dark, secret sex of Orleans.

The fireplace roars suddenly to life; I start violently.

He gives an artless shrug and smiles like a child, his finger still at the button on the wall. In the firelight, his hawk like beauty swells and fills the room. It makes the air heavy and languid.

He removes his jacket carefully and spreads it over the back of the couch. His shirt is loose, untucked at the waist, and one shoulder is bare. He folds his arms as he turns away from me and gazes into the cavernous fireplace.

The scent of jasmine rolls off of him in waves.

He is crying again.

I approach him from behind, the dark silhouette of this man-boy, gracefully long of leg and slender of limb, and I pull him back against me. I rest my chin between his shoulder blades and breathe in his scent. He continues to cry. I rub my cheek against his hair; his hands cover mine.

"Don't cry," I tell him.

"I don't want to *die*," he intones, voice smoky.

"I don't understand--"

He pulls away from me, his face a roadmap of black rivers.

"Even now, you *lie* to me!"

He is sobbing.

"But you *love* me, I'm certain of that..."

He reaches for my hand and traces the lines in my palm with one finger. I allow him to lead me to the couch.

"You *aren't* my first, you know," he murmurs with a wry smile. His eyes catch mine and hold them. I am lost in his and quite unable to reply.

He stands, and removes his trousers, revealing black satin high-cuts, garters, and black seamed stockings. I go to him, and he raises his arms and allows me to pull the billowy, satin shirt over his head. It floats gracefully to the floor, already forgotten.

He smiles then, his beautiful teeth flashing as lightning streaks the sky at the window behind him. He glances back over his shoulder at it, then again fixes me in his warm gaze. There is a playful gleam in his eye.

The scales are now balanced. He was my prisoner, and now I am his. We are frozen in time, frozen with rapture.

He seizes me very suddenly, through my trousers. His leather-clad hand is warm and slippery.

I ache with the want of him, and struggle to check the orgasm which threatens to defeat me.

This is a grievous challenge indeed.

Talk about singing for your supper.

What an extraordinary human specimen he is! He pouts, and looks at me shyly. His mouth looks engorged, ripe, appallingly so, almost as if his lips would burst with blood at my touch.

As if in answer to my question, he bites his lower lip like a naughty child, and a thin trickle of blood begins its slow trail down his chin.

Surprisingly, I'm not hungry. Odd.

I take him by the shoulders, then press my cheek against his and nuzzle his ear. I explore his hip, buttock and leg with one hand, and thrust my fingers deeply into the top of his stocking.

He groans, an otherworldly sound, and bends his leg at the knee as he rests his boot clad foot on the couch behind me.

I take him gently into the palm of my hand. He gasps, his lips near my ear. I pull back to look at him, I touch his face, my fingers fan out over his cheek.

He is so beautiful.

I kiss his lips; he kisses mine.

His lips are soft and full, and his mouth seems full of honey...but he is all fire, his tongue is quick.

We make our way to the back room, limbs entangled.

I collapse backwards on the bed, my hair fanning out beneath me. He slides my trousers off my long thighs, slowly and torturously, until I think that I'm about to die. I feel his breath on my skin, warm and wet, as he trails soft butterfly kisses over my pelvic bones and beneath my belly.

"All *right* then," he purrs, licks his lips, and takes me deep into his mouth. He is a skilled lover, and stops just before I'm ready to climax. He grasps my hands, pulls me up into a sitting position, and rests his foot on the bed beside me. I unzip the boot, and wrap my fingers around his ankle, gradually moving upwards, my fingers tracing the seam. He moves his leg to my shoulder, holding on to me for balance.

'*Neat trick, I'll have to remember that one,*' I'm thinking as my tongue replaces my fingertips at the stocking seam.

He is straining at the front of his high cuts,

I free him by releasing the catch at his hip.

Now, he stands before me in all of his alabaster abundance. He is beautiful like milk...*like cream.*

His dark eyes are burning holes in my soul.

I grasp his hips and draw him close to me.

He bares his teeth and hisses as my tongue explores the length of him; he whimpers as the pleasure begins to build.

My hands move to his buttocks and squeeze gently.

"*Easy,*" he whispers, "Lie back."

I do as he commands, and he climbs on top of me. His lips meet mine, and he forces my mouth open with his tongue. We kiss for what seems like hours, his body warm and electric against mine. He feels good in my arms, fits me like a glove.

Finally, he releases my mouth and snuggles his head under my arm; I take his hand and pull his arm across my belly. He smiles against my flesh, and rubs my chest with his fingertips.

At last, he takes me in his hand and begins a slow, delicious friction. It results in an orgasm which threatens my very ties with the present world...

I scream, my arms reaching out in vain for a grasp on reality...and suddenly, he is there again...my arms are full, my heart sings with joy.

My hands are in his hair, his lips on mine. I push him onto his back; he is panting. He is in my hand, trembling all over, and he erupts.

He cries out, as if in pain.

I sit beside him; I stroke his brow, as I bring him back, little by little.

Slowly, his eyes swim back into focus and connect with mine. He is tired, I can see that.

I touch my lips to his temple softly, and his eyelids flutter. I reach out to him mentally, and open the walls of his mind completely.

He shudders wordlessly, and I walk through...

~*~*~*~

I am in a room filled with cut jasmine blossoms. He is at my side, holding my arm. I look at him.

"You're afraid."

He lifts his chin and glances upwards.

"I don't want to die," he intones yet again. His lips barely move as he speaks, and a lone tear trickles down one cheek.

"Yes," I reply rather sharply, "So you say."

He turns to me, face pained.

"You mock me," he groans, his voice husky with tears.

My heart aches for him.

"No, my Darling. Don't do this," I plead. He turns away from me. "Can we talk about this?"

He ignores me, lost in his own world of pain.

I start to reach for him, but the hunger is beginning to rear its cruel head.

"I'm leaving," I announce abruptly, and instantly find myself at his bedside once more.

~*~*~*~

I look down at his pallid face upon the pillow.

He is relaxed, but there's a small crease of anxiety between his brows. I press my lips to it, and momentarily, it disappears. I take his hand in mine and hold it gently. His fingers squeeze mine, and his lashes--long, sooty, and naturally black--flutter like cremation ashes in the breeze from the open window. He dimples prettily, and pouts.

"Don't go, don't *leave* me..."

I do not wish to move from his side, but the hunger is roaring up from my very depths.

He is in great danger.

"Darling, please release me! I shall return momentarily! This I *vow*!"

His lips tremble, and he whispers:

"They *all* leave...they leave me here to suffer alone..." His voice breaks "...and I *loved* every one of them!"

He cries.

My heart moves toward him. I'm afraid to hold him; the hunger is consuming me, dirtying my veins like heroin. Soon, I will know not what I do.

"I must leave you *now!*" I utter urgently, trying to pull away, but he is clutching my arm tightly. "Have mercy, I *must* go!!!"

His eyes are warm brown, rimmed with tears. He pulls me to his chest and looks at me steadily.

"I *know* what you are," he intones. "I don't *care.*"

I try to pull away, but he won't release me.

"*Look* at me," he pleads, "I can't live without you!"

He presses his lips to mine, they are trembling.

[9]

He is trembling.

So am *I*.

"*Take* me," he murmurs against my lips. "Take me with you." His tongue parts my lips, I taste sweet honey.

The roar of the blood under his flesh deafens me.

He is *lost*.

With all my will, I fight it. I struggle, my body already making the journey, my mind following fast. I embrace him fully, my lips at his ear.

"Are you *certain* about this?"

A faint scent of jasmine.

I pull back to look at him.

He gasps.

My mouth has grown deep with teeth.

Trembling, eyes wide, lips softly parted, he regards me with terror.

"*Yes*, then," I whisper. My voice is like a growl.

He is catatonic with fear.

I am quite beyond mercy at this point. I brush his cheek with my lips, kiss him deeply, and lay him back.

His hair is splashed out around his head like black ink on the silken white sheets. His eyes never leave my face.

He is beautiful, his soft white flesh shining in the moonlight like a marble slab of a holy altar, his lips as red as the blood of a sacrificial lamb.

I trace the line of his body with one fingertip, as I throw back my head once again, and listen to the night...

There is a quiet in Orleans, a *whispering*.

He is trembling.

I trail my fingertips over the curve of his hip, and up his side, and then rest my palm over his heart. It feels like the fluttering of a caged, doomed bird.

He gasps as I bend over him and push my tongue into the hollow at the base of his throat.

His hand comes up to cradle the back of my head.

His flesh is cold with terror.

I lift him back up against me, my hands spread across his chest. His head hangs forward; he is exhausted, near a faint. With one arm, I take a stray strand of his brilliant ebony hair in my fingertips and move it out of the way.

He murmurs wordlessly as I lick his ear, then raises his face to the heavens and covers my hands with his own.

"I'm so *cold,*" he whispers, as I rest my cheek between his shoulder blades.

His hair (was there *ever* such hair?) silkens my cheek and brow...I can hear his heartbeat, accelerated with terror.

I feel a rush of the hunger so intensely, my vision blurs, and I emit a low moan. He turns to me, his beautiful face filled with sorrow.

"It's *okay,*" he says, weeping silently, his eyes bright, and yet very dark. "*Take* me," he begs, offering his smooth, white throat. "I cannot live like this anymore."

I cradle his cheek in my hand, lift his jaw aside with my thumb, and tuck my head under his chin to the promise of his silken white throat.

"I love you so much," he sobs, and leans his cheek against the top of my head...

...And suddenly, we are not alone.

Chapter Three

He raises his head, his eyes widen. He gasps.

"Timothy!"

"Brian???"

Annoyed, I turn from my Brian (so that's his name; how *odd* that I didn't ask) and see a young man of about our age, leaning against the doorframe with his arms crossed. He is clearly a prostitute, in our style of dress, and very handsome with beautiful lips, silken chestnut hair, and feline eyes as green and unforgiving as the stained glass in a cathedral window. He is tapping his stiletto boot rapidly against the floor, and his lips are drawn back in disgust.

"Well???" he demands, clacking that goddamned boot even louder until I want to drench him in kerosene and set him on fire.

Brian, *my* Brian, my beautiful beloved, embraces me fully, and kisses my mouth, teeth and all.

"I *love* him," Brian pouts. "Go away."

"Is that what he told you?" Timothy sneers at me, his Creole accent thick and deep. "You have a lot to learn. *That* one only takes what he wants, and uses others for his own survival!"

Brian is quietly sobbing, trembling in my arms.

My lips thin into a sneer.

Timothy gives us an uneasy glance, and then his lips tighten in disgust.

"Well, *have* 'im, then," he ejaculates, and stalks back through the house on long, stockinged legs, his heels clacking on the floor as he retreats. "You're *nothing!!!"* he calls back. "You're *worthless!"*

He starts back towards the bedroom, where Brian is still crying, and rocking back and forth with pain.

"You'd rather *die* than live with me???" He seizes Brian's arm and shakes him. "To the *devil* with you, then! Do you *hear* me, Brian??? To the *devil!!!"*

His voice breaks.

"To the *devil...*"

Rage swells within me, and I am upon Timothy in two tenths of a second. I take him from behind, yank his head back roughly from his silken locks, and bare my teeth.

"To the *devil*, you say? Good plan!"

His death cry is quickly cut short; there is a spray of blood, coppery and sweet, as my teeth make their fatal journey and meet deep within his flesh.

Brian gives a cry and turns away in fright and disgust.

The blood bursts into my mouth, warm and salty over my tongue. I am enraptured, my own blood sings with the excited joy of the chase, and the satisfaction of a job well done.

When I am sated, I lift Timothy's body in my arms and lay it on the couch. I cover his head with Brian's jacket, and then go back to the side of my precious love. I find him sitting on the bed, fingering his own throat, lips trembling.

"Darling, *no*," I soothe, but he won't look at me. He is staring straight ahead. "Brian, my *love!"*

His cheeks are damp with tears.

"Sweetheart," I try, but he flinches when I try to touch him.

Suddenly, I am furious.

"Brian, he was just a *vessel*. He lived eighty years of life in twenty years and eight months--"

"He was a human being!" Brian cries. "The only one who loved me, but I didn't *want* him. I didn't *love* him. Not that way."

I go to him and hold him, he seated, I kneeling.

"Brian, come here." I grasp his chin gently with my fingertips. He regards me with unhappy eyes, and then looks down at his hands lying helplessly in his lap.

"There is a natural order to things that *be,"* I explain. "It may seem cruel, but nature itself is both cruel and kind, black and white, good and evil. Do you follow?" He nods. "Good."

I pull away from him and start pacing the floor.

"I was trying to leave earlier so that I could *spare* you this hideous sight! I almost took you instead! If Timothy hadn't come in, it would have been *you*! Is that really what you wanted?"

He begins to cry in earnest then, and I am grievously sorry that I have hurt him.

"You are my *heart*," I tell him, taking his hands in mine. "It scares me to be so close to a mere mortal. *Love*? I did not know the meaning of the word until tonight! Do you realize how *extraordinary* you are?"

His eyes meet mine. He looks guilty. I'm puzzled.

"I'm not extraordinary, I'm *not*. I sell my body for..." His voice trails off. I cradle his cheek in my hand.

"*Dream maker*," I smile tenderly. "You sell *dreams*. You weave your dream threads through the minds of men. You are fantasy. *Ecstasy*. You are the toast of Orleans."

"*Really*? Thank you."

"You're welcome; now help me with Timothy's body. Morning is coming quickly."

Chapter Four

Together, we wrap Timothy's body in a sheet, and carry it between us. It is a common enough sight, with the sickness cutting through the city of Orleans with the sharpness and finality of the reaper's scythe. Instead of pausing at the house of the local undertaker, or at the hospital, we continue our journey into the trees at the outskirts of town.

The ground is soft, moist, rich with minerals, and fragrant. I notice Brian struggling with the body, and we cease. His eyes meet mine, and his lower lip trembles a bit. This has been a traumatic night for him.

I laugh at myself, feeling such a connection to a mere mortal. I never would have believed that I would fall in love with anyone, let alone a prostitute, no matter how beautiful. After all, love is Brian's business, and he is adept at creating a wall of illusion to suit his many clients. He has taken me for sure.

Momentarily, an odd thought crosses my mind: '*Should I kill him? Is this all another illusion, thrown over me like the silken, yet deadly threads of a spider's web to entrap me?*' I gaze at him warily as he begins to drive the spade into the earth with his boot. He is covered with a light film of grime and sweat.

His hair is drawn back and fastened at the back of his neck with a black velvet ribbon, but a few strands have escaped to hang artlessly about his hollow cheeks and over his fine, high brow. After a moment, he notices me staring at him, and pouts.

"Aren't you going to help?"

Without a word, I take up another spade and begin to turn the earth. What a goddamned *bother* these mortals make out of death! I have always left my victims to be found by others. In a bizarre form, it is a gesture of respect that I show to the living. Let them have their *ceremony*, their *rituals*, and their prayers to a nonexistent god. It comforts them, prepares them, for the horrors and catastrophes of everyday existence.

Brian startles me out of my reverie by throwing the spade at my feet.

"What is *wrong* with you? Hurry up!"

Rage swells up within me like gasoline on a fire, and I slap him with the full force of my arm across the face.

Blood trickles from his nose. He sobs quietly, and looks at his feet. Timothy's body is about six inches from his left boot. He sinks to his knees, and undrapes Timothy's face. His chestnut hair is still silken, and his features are as sharp as the edge of a knife under the moon. He touches his lips to Timothy's brow, his eyelids, his mouth.

"I'm *sorry*," he weeps. "I'll love you *now.*" He pulls the body up into his arms and sobs into Timothy's hair as if his heart is breaking.

I give him a moment, and then I seize the body and toss it roughly into the chasm. As I begin to fill in the grave, I can feel Brian's hatred of me.

Worse, the scent of jasmine hangs in the air once more, like an accusation.

I *hate* myself. I am solely the cause of Brian's pain.

I finish the job, and take up the spades as I prepare to leave.

"Are you coming?" I ask softly.

"I'll be along," he intones.

I sigh wearily. "So be it."

It takes all of my will to turn and leave Brian, but oddly, I feel that it is the right thing to do.

Soon, I find myself in the city once more. It is very quiet, being exactly one hour from the dawn. I will never make it back to my dark apartment in time, this I know. I head for Brian's domain quickly, tucking my chin down into the collar of my long leather coat.

'*Yes, it is a bit much for a sultry Orleans evening, but, oh--we must be dashingly fashionable or die.*' I grin, enjoying the absurdity of my own train of thought, and run head on into a tall, slim, graceful redhead with large, soulful eyes and a shy smile.

"*Benediction*," I smile, genuinely delighted. He is a vision in a white lace, three piece suit, white blousy shirt, and creamy knee boots made of suede with stiletto heels. He is fair of cheek, fresh-faced and innocent, soft-spoken. But far the most remarkable features are the snowy white wings trailing from his back.

"*Hey*, Matthias," he greets me. "How goes the hunt? A little *late* for you, isn't it?"

"I was just finishing up."

"Best to get indoors, then."

"All *right*, I hear you," I laugh, as he turns and walks away, hips twitching prettily. Brian appears beside me, and his eyes follow mine to Benediction's pert backside.

"So, who is *he?*" Brian asks, his voice so cold that the words crack like ice in the night air.

I touch his cheek; the skin is an angry red where I slapped him. He closes his eyes and bows his head. His raven hair frames his face like shining curtains.

"Who *is* he?" His voice trembles.

"Just an old friend," I reassure him, lifting his chin and pressing my lips to his. I encircle him with my arm, and we walk home.

Chapter Five

On arrival at Brian's home, he quickly pulls the drapes and puts on a kettle for tea. There is a knock at the door. I move to the back room to avoid the faint slivers of light which poke through the doorframe like scorching glass.

"Yes, what is it?" Brian's voice from the next room is tense and low.

"Terribly sorry to trouble you, but is Matthias Ste. Germain about? It's urgent that we speak."

"Who???" Brian demands. I have never told him my name.

"I'm *here*, Beni'! Get in here and close that goddamned door!" I call, as I gaze into the mirror over the bathroom vanity and strive to make myself presentable.

A difficult task.

I am covered in grime, my hair is greasy and tangled, and my mouth feels sour and unclean. I brush my teeth, urinate, and after a quick, circumspective sniff under one arm, run a bath. After all, just because I'm fully a man in every way, doesn't mean that I have an obligation to stink like a savage beast.

I smile at myself in the mirror, feeling silly and slightly giddy, as if with champagne. I shut off the bathtub tap and sink into a tub full of fragrant bubbles.

Bubbles.

I can't help it this time; I throw back my head and laugh heartily, slopping filthy water all over the floor.

Beni' watches me from the doorway, his innocent face beaming with mischief, his kind eyes amused.

Brian is *not* amused...he's clearly annoyed. He eyes the dirty clothes and towels on the vanity, the sink which is covered with blood and grime, and the water soaked floor. "Oh, *barf*!" he spits, and pouts. Beni' chuckles.

I flush a deep red, and sink below the water's surface to wet my hair. I want them *both* to go away.

No such luck.

Beni' perches on the edge of the old fashioned tub, and waits for me to resurface. Brian folds his arms and scowls.

Shit. I have to breathe. There's no escape. The fucking Scylla and Charybdis have nothing on these two.

I break the surface with an audible gasp, and the two of them stare at me.

"Matthias, what in the *world---?"* Beni' grins, shaking his head. I clear my throat, reach behind me for a towel, and step out of the tub.

"Gentlemen." I clear my throat again, swallow hard, and fasten the towel around my slim hips.

"Matty, I must speak to you. Urgently."

I grab a comb and pull it through my long, black hair. "So, *speak* then."

When Benediction remains silent, I turn to him. His face alarms me. He is suddenly filled with a dark, terrible beauty.

"Your friend is in grave danger. The two of you were seen carrying a shrouded corpse into the woods. We must *go,"* Benediction says, turning to Brian. He holds out his hand, but Brian backs away.

"Fuck off," he snarls, "Who *are* you, anyway?"

Beni' looks back at him steadily. "Now is not the time. We must leave."

"I'm *not* leaving Matthias." He ducks under my arm and encircles my waist loosely in his arms.

I squeeze his shoulder and kiss his brow softly. *"Shhhh,* listen to Beni'."

"Time is *short,"* Benediction urges Brian. "We must flee!"

"It's okay," I tell Brian. "Go on. I will come after you later."

Brian's eyes plead with mine, but I am reading the psychic replay in Benediction's mind. It opens up like a cinema screen before my eyes. Obadiah...

~*~*~*~

A group of about ten men are knocking on doors a few blocks away. They have already made two "arrests", and the

[14]

two prostitutes are being pushed along ahead of the crowd. It is an ugly procession. The two men have been badly beaten, and they struggle along, wrists bound painfully with duct tape, bodies clothed in black hooded robes.

This scene is also the norm in Orleans. Death processions. Vigilante justice. No trial of any legal sort. One moment, a person is safe in their home; the next, they're severed from this world by some of the most violent means possible.

I know both of the men in the hoods. One, a tall blond with round blue eyes and distinctly Scandinavian features, and the other, a slim, brown haired youth with a solemn and beautiful face.

Both are frightened, for they know that it is the end for them, but they don't tremble. Rather, the blond is angry, the brunette, serene.

Two of the rabble step forward and remove the hoods from the heads of the two condemned men. The crowd falls into a hushed silence, moved by the beauty of these innocent victims.

The blond, Arik, holds his proud, leonine head high. The brunette, Noah, has his eyes fixed on some distant, faraway point, past life all a memory now.

All at once, the crowd moves to either side, and a tall figure clad in a shining white robe appears, sword in hand. He is cruelly beautiful. His long, fair hair undulates in the wind like a flag around his pale, handsome face. His dark green eyes are piercing, and glint like obsidian.

He is Obadiah, and his name is synonymous with terror in the French Quarter. A former prostitute who claims that he "found God" two years hence, and a self-appointed purveyor of justice, he has cut a bloody swath through the community of the 'Gypsy Boys', as they are affectionately named. Although he claims to be a man of God, he carries an aura of supernatural strength about him.

Obadiah approaches the blond, who glares at him. He grin is vulpine and repulsive.

"Arik...we found Timothy's body outside of town."

"Timothy? It was Tim?" A tear courses down his cheek.

Obadiah chuckles darkly.

"Now, Arik...I know you don't expect for me to believe that you're surprised..." He puts his lips to Arik's ear. "I know that you're a murderer and a whore...do you want to add 'liar' to your list of sins as well?" He walks behind him. "You already have much to atone for."

Arik lifts his chin with quiet dignity.

"I did not kill Tim. I did no such thing. He was a friend."

"A friend," Obadiah sneers. "A friend, indeed! I know what friends do in your circle...all you do is kill and fuck, fuck and kill..." Obadiah is shaking with righteous anger, his voice rising "...and what of you, Noah?" he addresses the brunette, who does not respond, but continues to stare into the distance. "Really, Noah...you have nothing to say?"

No reply.

"Then you are cursed." His voice is soft, but ridden with underlying malice. The crowd murmurs, rapt and electric.

Obadiah's face is contorted with rage; the large crystal and ivory cross around his neck burns with an unholy light in the sun.

He raises his arms and the sword to the sky.

"Why, God? Why won't they repent? Why do you make me do this?" He turns to walk away...then the sword makes its deadly arc, and Noah's head falls to the ground. There is a great fountain of blood, and the body collapses at Obadiah's feet.

"You monster," Arik snarls.

"Monster?" Obadiah chuckles. "You are the monster, my love--"

"What would you know about love?" Arik shouts. "You claim to be a man of God, but isn't one of his main commandments 'Thou--Shalt--Not--KILL???!!!'"

The crowd gasps, and there is much muttering. Arik's eyes are boring holes into Obadiah's, and they shine like twin orbs of fire.

It is now a battle of will.

Obadiah raises the sword over his head.

The world fills with a bright light, and Benediction appears between Obadiah and Arik.

"No!!!" Benediction commands, and there is a flash of light as the sword falls from Obadiah's hand.

Obadiah screams, the seared flesh still smoking.

"NO MORE! HE IS INNOCENT!!!" Benediction thunders. Arik sways, collapses. Benediction catches him under the arms and pulls him to his chest, encircling him with his arms, and with his snow white wings. He whispers softly to Arik, and begins to sing. It is a beautiful sound, reminiscent of bells, harps, crystal, twinkling stars...the air shimmers around them.

When Benediction's wings are opened once again, Arik's bruises are gone, his cuts healed. His snowy blond hair, long and flowing and shorn at the sides, is silky and clean. His beautiful alabaster face is radiant; his lips are full and red. His crystal blue eyes are shining with joy.

Benediction's lips brush his brow gently, and he clothes him in black velvet trousers, patent platforms, and a blousy, billow-sleeved black shirt which laces at the neck.

"BEHOLD!" Benediction shouts, his voice loud and clear. "BEHOLD! I MAKE ALL THINGS NEW!!!"

He embraces Arik once more...

~*~*~*~

Brian jumps with fright as Benediction and Arik appear in front of us, and a faint scent of jasmine emits. Beni' tucks back his wings, and Arik looks about in confusion.

"Brian? How...*what--?"* He breaks down. "Oh, Brian, Timothy and Noah are dead...Obadiah--" Arik sees me, and falls silent.

"Matty, what's happening?" Brian gasps. "You looked so strange, and Beni' disappeared, and how did Arik--?"

Tears are coursing down Brian's cheeks. I kiss them away, and smooth his hair with the palm of my hand.

"Arik, what of Obadiah?" Brian whimpers, his voice muffled against my chest.

"He pulled me out of my front garden. He had quite a few men with him. Rough types, you know. The men who hate us. They beat me...cursed my soul, spit on me. They taped my hands together and paraded me down the street...and they had Noah. You know, the little brunette with the sad eyes? He wouldn't speak...they had beaten him too. It was as if his soul had already fled. He was an empty shell." Arik swallows hard, and shudders. "Obadiah beheaded him with a sword."

"He was only fourteen," Brian says softly. There is a silence.

"Brian, he would have killed me too, had Benediction not intervened."

Brian turns to Benediction, and regards him in awe.

"Who *are* you?" he asks, his voice soft with wonder.

Beni' smiles then, and allows Brian to see his wings for the first time. Brian releases me and goes to Beni', and stands before him, staring, his lips softly parted. He reaches out and touches one of Beni's wings with his fingertips.

A faint scent of jasmine hangs lightly in the air, both from Brian and Arik. They do not understand.

"Come, my Children," Benediction smiles, embracing both Brian and Arik. "I will explain."

"But Beni'!" I exclaim. "Obadiah--"

"They are out of danger this day at least, Matty," he assures me, and a soft, white light fills the room. Under his wing, Brian is radiant. His glorious, raven mane is once again smooth and shining, his alabaster skin is glowing and clean, and his lips are red as rose petals. Best of all, his eyes are shining with happiness. He is as beautiful as a god, if such a thing were to exist.

I feel that familiar pull in my chest, the one the mortals call love. I long for him, his supple body, his voice, his lips on mine, his hair in my hands...

"We will speak soon," Beni' smiles at me with gentle understanding. "But Arik and Brian need sleep." He winks at me. I blush, miserable.

Chapter Six

We put Arik and Brian to bed. Beni' sits by Arik's side, and I, at Brian's. I smile down at Brian tenderly, and stroke his cheek with the back of my hand. I gaze at Benediction, who is smoothing Arik's hair back from his brow.

"He's *sick,*" Beni says sadly. "He nearly died today, and he's very weak right now."

Guilt is a new emotion for me, but it wells up as I look into Arik's face. He is so pale, the blood vessels can be seen under his skin, and two red splotches of fever stretch over his cheeks. All of a sudden, Arik's eyes focus intently on Beni's face.

"Benediction...are you *God?*"

Beni' smiles gently. "No, my Darling."

Brian yawns, stretches, and turns over to face Beni'. "Well, who are you then?" He tucks his hands under his cheek, and his eyes meet Beni's. "I mean, you're an angel, right?"

Benediction's face has a soft, wondrous smile, and a light seems to glow in his eyes as he drinks in Brian's sensuality. He touches Brian's shoulder, his hair, the side of his face, his head tilted to one side. "Beautiful boy," he says warmly. "I am an angel of sorts, but not as you think." Beni' sighs deeply, lost in thought.

"Long ago, when the world was newly formed, my kind were created for the purpose of companionship to a certain deity. This deity was, at that time, a great and wondrous power. We loved IT, and IT loved us. But over time, this deity grew cold, selfish, paranoid, and corrupt. IT committed great atrocities against those who worshipped IT, and my kind watched fearfully in the shadows, helpless to react. Soon, the tests of faith came, and humankind was in turmoil upon the Earth. Everywhere, there was war, sickness, great strife. At last, I decided to speak to IT; to try to reason with IT, to tell IT what IT was doing was wrong..."

Benediction's breath catches in his throat, and his eyes are wet.

"Before I knew what happened, my friends and I were cast out of Heaven, and hurled to the Earth."

"So, God *does* exist?" Brian asks, rapt.

"It's...complicated," Beni' replies. "Gods *die*, you see. They need men to worship them, because they live in their minds and their hearts. Otherwise, they grow weak, and eventually fade away. That deity that I have spoken of is dead, and rightfully so."

"So, where is Timothy now?" Brian whispers, his eyes shimmering, "And where is Noah?"

"Timothy and Noah are *dead*, Brian," Benediction says as gently as possible, "But they live in *here,*" he says, touching Brian's temple, "And in *here.*" He touches Brian's chest gently. "And there, they will never die."

"I want Timothy."

"You *have* Timothy," Benediction tries, his face lined with sorrow. "He's with you always."

Brian frowns. "You can't lay your hands on him and heal him?"

Beni' shakes his head.

"Why *not???!*" Brian demands.

"BECAUSE I AM *NOT* A DEITY!" Benediction shouts very suddenly. "I *cannot* create life where none exists!"

"Then what *good* are you?" Brian replies wearily, and turns his back.

I flash Benediction an apologetic look, and rub Brian's back as he sobs into the pillow.

Arik groans, uncomfortable with the fever that is climbing in his body.

"*Benediction*," I state, and gesture to Arik, but for once, Beni' looks desolate, lost, utterly powerless.

His eyes scare me.

"*Benediction*," I repeat sharply, "Beni', *stop* it. He didn't mean it."

"Yes, he did. He meant every word. He's right. I'm useless."

"Oh, *Beni'*..." His snow white wings are drooping, and a few of the feathers have fluttered to the floor. He has new lines around his eyes and mouth; he has aged. "Benediction, you have to *fight* this!"

Beni' is shaking all over. "I healed Arik, and he still doesn't *believe* in me."

"*Lucifer*," I state, addressing him by his formal name. "Lucifer, you must stop this immediately!"

"*Don't* call me that," Beni' groans. "I am *not* that person, I'm not who IT said that I was."

"I *know* that you're not, Beni'," Arik gasps. Beni's eyes soften a bit, and he takes Arik's hands firmly in the two of his.

"Don't worry yourself, my child," Benediction smiles, kissing his cheek. "Be at peace."

Arik's eyes close, and his breathing is slow and steady once more. I notice that Brian has also fallen asleep.

Beni' rises from the bedside, and leaves the room without a word. I stroke Brian's hair with the palm of my hand, then follow Beni' into the kitchen.

He is sitting at the table with a glass of white wine. He has been badly shaken.

Briefly, I wonder if this is to be my fate, to poison and corrupt all those who love me. I wonder about ending myself...is suicide an option for an immortal?

Suddenly, I feel Benediction inside my mind, behind my psychic wall. I glance up at him. He is not pleased.

"Don't be *stupid*, Matthias," he mutters into his glass as he finishes the wine and pours himself another. He smiles crookedly at me, and gulps down yet another glass. "And don't look at me like that," he laughs, but there is absolutely no humor in his tone.

"Something more is bothering you," I tell him, as he hands me a glass of wine, and fills his own cup again.

"Perhaps," he mumbles, his speech slurring. "I lied. I could have saved Noah...and I *could* resurrect them both."

"Then why don't you? Brian would be so happy---"

"No, he wouldn't. Brian would feel obligated to Timothy. Where would that leave the two of you?"

"Thanks, Beni'...now I really *do* hate myself."

"That wasn't the point. How do you think that Timothy would react to having *you* around? If he is resurrected, he will remember his death, and all of the events leading up to it."

I sink down in my chair and put my head in my hands. I have a lot to think through.

Chapter Seven

Evening comes around all too soon, and I am still badly torn. A part of me thinks that I should just walk away into the night and spare him further pain, but my heart won't let me leave him.

I smile at the beautiful boy with whom I've fallen in love, reflected in the mirror beside me, and realize how truly extraordinary he is. Not many people could see what he did earlier and remain sane, but my Brian has proven to be surprisingly resilient, although I suspect that he's hurting deep down inside of himself.

"Matt," Beni' beckons from the doorway. "Come."

I reluctantly tear my eyes away from Brian, who is attaching a garter to the seamed black stocking encasing his long, slim leg, and bite my lip.

"Damned Benediction..." I mumble, and it suddenly hits me funny. "*Damned*...damned straight!" I stifle a bubble of laughter, and Brian looks up at me in mock annoyance.

"You're *so* weird," he grins, and goes back to straightening his seam. I can feel my body responding to him, but I pull back and follow Beni' into the sitting room instead.

Beni' pours a full goblet of wine for me, then one for himself. "Sit," he tells me.

I roll my eyes.

"Oh, for fuck's sake, not this shit again!" I groan, and throw myself backwards into a chair by the fireplace like a sulky teen. Beni' raises his eyebrows at me.

"Are you *through*?"

"Are you *sober*???" I fire back at him, and then I realize that I'm being unfair. "I'm *sorry*, Benediction. Please go on."

"Shove it up your *ass*, Matty," Beni' snarls--quite out of character--and stalks out of the room.

I stare after him, gulp down the wine in both glasses, and head back to the bathroom, only to find Brian and Beni' deep in conversation.

Shit. This can't be good.

I hesitate for a moment, then go to the bedroom, where Arik is sitting up in bed, eating some mushy concoction of crackers and what looks like chicken dumpling stew. It looks vile, and smells worse. However, Arik looks much better, which is what is important, I guess.

"You're eating, that's an improvement," I tell him, feeling rather awkward, although we have known each other completely in the not so distant past.

He smiles. "I'm better," he tells me, his blue eyes studying me intently. "Benediction saved my life."

"You're *lucky*. He rarely intervenes."

Arik sets the bowl aside, and looks down at his hands in his lap. "He could have saved Noah."

"Perhaps," I reply. "But he didn't save Timothy."

"If I beg him, he may."

I put my arm around him, and he leans into me.

"You know that Beni' is out of sorts today."

I inhale deeply, and sigh. "No shit."

"I heard him speaking to Brian just before you came in." His round blue eyes catch mine and hold them. "He was talking about Timothy, about resurrection. Brian was giving him the third degree---"

No, no, no. Beni' isn't that angry with me...or is he? I leap up and race into the bathroom, only to find Brian in Benediction's arms, weeping.

"*What* in the *Hell* are you trying to *do*???" I demand, pushing Benediction back against the sink and grabbing him by the throat with one hand.

"*STOP IT!*" Brian cries. "*Both* of you!!!"

Benediction uses the advantage of surprise to slap my face soundly. I snarl, and tighten my grip on his throat.

"I *said*, STOP!!!" Brian screams, stamping his booted foot hard.

We both ignore him, silent and fierce in our anger.

[19]

Brian grabs the glass from the sink and hurls it to the floor, where the crystal shatters in a million pieces. The sound is as effective as a gunshot. Benediction and I stare dumbly at him.

"Good. Now I know that you're listening." He comes to me, grasps my hips to pull me close to him, and then throws his arms around my neck and smiles happily.

"Benediction has offered to try to resurrect Timothy." He kisses my cheek and laughs.

"Beni', how *could* you?" I cry. "*Why* would you do such a thing? You know how these things turn out."

Beni' smiles grimly. "You mean like falling in love with a *mortal?*"

"Beni', I'm sorry that I hurt you earlier," Brian says softly, and goes to him to kiss his cheek. "Please forgive me."

Benediction's wings, which were drooping before, lift up off the ground, and his face instantly loses every trace of anger.

"Of *course* I forgive you, my beautiful child," he says gently.

I am so filled with joy to see Benediction back to his old self; I throw my arms around him as well. His arm encircles my waist, and he pulls both Brian and me close to him. It feels good to hold him, for a good friend is more vital than blood.

"*Arik,*" Benediction remembers, and the three of us go to him. Arik is looking at all of us rather strangely, and he notices the tears on our faces.

"What's wrong? Did someone else die?"

Benediction smiles brightly, his face like the sun. "No," he laughs. "No, just the opposite. Now get dressed."

Chapter Eight

We are a strange sight, the four of us. People are used to seeing Brian and Arik's type about, and the two of them have an air of joy around them which is mesmerizing. Beni' and myself are harder for them to figure out. Although Beni's wings are invisible to the mortal eye, he has a fresh-faced but wise look to him.

'It's in the eyes,' I think to myself, *'Those fathomless eyes, as endless as time.'*

Brian and Arik walk ahead of us. Side by side, they are almost like photo negatives. Both are extremely fair complected, but Brian's straight, waist length black hair contrasts sharply with Arik's snowy blond layered spikes, which fall over his brow, arc softly upward, and then cascade in an icy waterfall down his back.

"Where is Timothy now?" Arik asks Benediction, as Beni' puts a gentle arm around his shoulders.

"They buried him in the common graveyard."

"The one behind the church? In *sacred* ground???" Brian grins, and then throws back his head and laughs. "Poor Timmy!"

"Brian, be more respectful," I scold, and Brian pouts.

"If you say so...but *you* killed--" He stops, and his expression is very strange, as if he is seeing me for the first time. I take his hand in mine, and he pulls away from me.

Oh, no.

I don't think that I can take this.

He knows that he has hurt me, and bites his lip, immediately sorry for what he has done...but what have I done to him?

Beni' senses my pain, and takes me under his warm, white, shining wing. I fight the urge to collapse into tears, and instead, snuggle my head on his shoulder. He releases Arik, and embraces me fully.

"What do I do *now?"* I whisper, my heart breaking. Beni' kisses my brow, and then rests his chin on the top of my head.

"What you've been doing all along. *Love* him."

I gaze over at Brian, who is speaking coquettishly to a rather odd-looking person. He is a young brunette, cute rather than handsome, with large, dark eyes and a beautiful mouth. His hair is long, pulled back from his face, and falls in long, curly tendrils to his waist. He is young, perhaps eighteen, no more. The oddness of which I speak comes from his clothing. He is dressed in a long, red robe...and white socks and sneakers.

I shudder. How *tacky*.

Brian smiles at him, and lowers his lashes. "A choir boy, eh?"

The boy smiles back, and begins to sing 'Gloria in Excelsis Deo', in a clear, beautiful alto.

I am enjoying it, but Beni's feathers are standing on end.

Arik leans back against the wall, bends one knee, and lights a cigarette. He surveys the pair of them with his icy gaze, and mutters, "Show us what's under the *robe*, then."

Still singing, the boy complies, and Brian laughs artlessly, clapping his hands. The boy is completely naked, and his skin is the color of coffee and cream. He is scarred badly all over, but the marks on his back are especially cruel. Despite that, he has a beauty of his own.

I cannot help staring, and the youth catches my eye and blushes. Sensing the boy's discomfort, Brian grasps the edges of the robe and pulls them back up around his shoulders. He whispers in his ear, then puts his arm around him and leads him back towards the house.

The feeling inside me is indescribable. I know better than to interfere, so I sulk instead. Beni' looks after them, but something is troubling him. Arik disappears into the shadows as well, arm in arm with one of his regulars.

"Benediction, is it *worth* resurrecting Timothy?" I ask, still snuggled against him. He sighs.

"Oh, Matthias...Tim means so much to Brian. They've been friends for many years. Tim is two years older..."

"So, Brian is--"

"*Eighteen.* Brian's parents died in a fire five years ago. They were his only family. Tim found him wandering the streets, half crazed with grief, and took him in. He taught him everything that he knew about the trade, and Brian excelled at it. He has a very innocent sensuality that men crave. He also has the gift of intuition, of sensing what his clients want...and of filling that need. He is a rare find, indeed."

He toys with a strand of my long, black hair for a moment, and smiles shyly.

"Brian and Arik are going to be a while," he tells me, "Do you want to go somewhere with me?" His eyes are beautiful: brown, hazel, gold and green, large and wide like morning glories...and his mouth is like a ripe strawberry. Bright strands of gingery red and gold hair fall softly over his brow and down over his shoulders, framing his fair face quite becomingly.

"Benediction...I-I don't know what to say!" I stammer. He touches my cheek.

"Then say nothing..." His lips brush mine twice, and he presses me close. "Matty, what a beauty you are..."

"Beni', *no*--that was a *long* time ago--" I protest, but his hands are already under my shirt, and my body is beginning to respond to his touch.

He murmurs into my ear, "Matty, *relax*..." and releases me. "We are *made* for each other, don't you see? We make *sense.* Brian will grow old and *die*, Matt."

"I don't *care!"* I cry, and turn my head when he tries to kiss me once more. His lips touch my ear, and I shiver. I feel Beni' in my mind, pushing against the psychic wall of my inhibitions, but I won't give in. Instead, I grab the telepathic link and fling back images of the previous night...Brian, Timothy's death, the gravesite.

We are locked into each other's minds so intently, that we don't hear Brian and Arik approach. They both look at us, then at each other, and Arik laughs.

"All *right*, Beni'!"

Brian looks at me with somber eyes. He looks like a wounded animal.

I know what it must look like. My shirt is open, and hanging out of my trousers, my hair is unkempt, and my face is smudged with Beni's coral tinted lip gloss.

Brian gives me his handkerchief without a word, and puts his arms around my waist. I can smell jasmine. He is miserable.

"You okay?" I whisper, as he presses his cheek to mine. He murmurs wordlessly.

Arik and Beni watch us for a moment, and then Arik speaks.

"Beni, can you really resurrect Tim?"

Beni looks at Arik solemnly. "I'll try."

The four of us walk together to the church, the night enveloping us like a cloak of black velvet.

Chapter Nine

We reach the church a few minutes later. It is well after midnight, and although the church doors are opened, the building is deserted. Beni and Arik make doubly sure, and Brian and I sit on one of the pews. He is quiet, somber. Brian's head is bowed, and his lips are moving silently. His beautiful hands, long fingered and slim like my own, are clasped together. I stare at him in disbelief for a moment, and then take his hands in mine. He raises his tear streaked face, and fresh agony is apparent in his eyes.

"Let me *pray*, Matty!"

I frown. "Stop this foolishness, Brian! Beni' told you what happened! IT is long dead!"

Brian weeps, and I hate myself more than ever.

My self-loathing is interrupted by a banging noise at the back of the church, where Beni' and Arik are lugging a filthy casket up onto the pulpit. They drop it heavily, and sit down beside it. Both of them are covered in dirt.

"He weighs a *ton*," Benediction complains, as Arik flops down beside him.

"It's all that damned muscle in his legs," Arik grumbles. "It weighs heavy."

Beni' embraces Arik in his wings, and both of them are clean again.

"So, what do you want to do about Noah?" Beni' asks Arik gently. "Do you want him resurrected too?" Arik thinks for a moment; his icy eyes hold a great sadness.

"No," he replies, "He was too young to understand what happened to him, or why. His soul had already fled before his death."

"So be it, then." Benediction opens the coffin and lifts Timothy's draped body into his arms. There is a beautiful bell-like singing in the air, and Benediction's eyes are like flames of fire. He lays Timothy's body on the altar, and lifts the sheet from his face, folding it at the waist. In death, Tim's features are softer: the catlike angles of his eyes, the broad, high cheekbones; the pale skin and long, silken chestnut hair are especially fine. His bottom lip has a sensual fullness to it that I hadn't noticed before, and I find myself wondering what his lips would taste like. *Persimmon*?

Benediction kisses Tim's brow, his nose, both cheeks, the palms of his hands, his chest, belly and feet. His wings arc out, magnificently white. He holds a dagger with a cut crystal hilt in one hand, a chalice in the other. I am familiar with this ritual, this ceremony...but Brian and Arik are emitting a scent of jasmine so strong, it's nearly overpowering. They're terrified.

Beni' begins speaking in Latin, and draws back his sleeve to the elbow. Brian clings to Arik; he trembles.

"It's *okay*," Arik reassures him, but he is frightened too.

Benediction is in a state of euphoria, lost in the tendrils of the old magic. It swirls around him in the form of colored light...white, blue, pink, green...the air shimmers and glistens with the voices of the past, both light and dark, the balance of nature. Beni' guides the blade across his own milky white wrist; the blood seeps to the surface and begins its slow trail to the chalice below. Arik is violently ill, and staggers to the back door with his hand over his mouth. There is a lot of blood.

Beni' allows himself to bleed until it is half full, and then holds out his hand toward Brian.

"*No!*" I protest. "Absolutely *not!*"

"There is no birth without *blood*, Matthias," Beni' smiles, eyes closed, face raised in rapture. "You know that as well as I do."

"But why *him*?" I demand angrily gesturing at Brian, who is cowering away from Beni'. "Hasn't he suffered enough?"

"*I'll* do it," a voice replies from the back door...

It's the curly haired youth from earlier tonight, the choir boy. I notice that he has changed into black jeans and a black button down shirt, and has ditched the white socks and sneakers for black boots. A noticeable improvement. His hair is unbound, and blows gently in the breeze from the door.

"Come in," I order him, "and shut the door behind you." He does as I command, and then spots Brian.

"Hey," he grins and waves, and I wait for Brian to cut him dead. Brian, to my surprise, rises and goes to him.

"Well, *hello*," Brian smiles. "Come to save me *again*, have you?"

Save him? What the fuck?

I shake it off, and turn my attention back to the altar, where Benediction is waiting patiently.

"*I'll* do it," I volunteer, and before Beni' can stop me, I seize the knife and cut my hand across the palm, adding my own blood to the mix.

"You realize what you've just done, do you not?" Beni' whispers, his voice low and tense. "He will rise, but he'll be one of yours, an immortal. The hunger will live in him."

"A small price to play," I mutter, and go to Arik, who is ashen-faced, sitting on the coffin.

"I want to give him my blood as well. Anything for Tim." Beni' leads him to the chalice, his wrist is slashed, the blood flows.

Beni' points to the boy in black, and he willingly presents his arm for the ritual cut. He groans, and tears squeeze out of the corners of his eyes.

Brian watches all of this, his arms folded. The air is heavy with jasmine once more. Strangely, the boy in black is perfectly calm, but Brian is terrified.

"Go *on*, Love," the boy says to Brian, who removes his jacket and pushes up his purple, blousy sleeve.

Beni' does it very quickly, heals our wounds, and the chalice is filled at last.

The singing grows louder, and Benediction's eyes are once again like twin flames of fire. He intones in Latin, and he sips from the chalice three times.

Blood.

Breath.

Body.

He dips his fingertips in the blood and anoints his brow, his lips, the hollow at the base of his neck, the palms of his hands, the top of his feet, his chest, and his genitals.

"*Sex* magic," the boy comments, and I stare at him.

Brian is trembling. The boy takes his hand, and Brian calms right away.

Benediction whispers, again lost in rapture, and dips the tip of the dagger in the blood. He hesitates, and then slips the blade under Tim's skin, at the base of his throat, and again between the ribs on his right side.

Brian whimpers, and the boy holds him.

Benediction pierces Tim's palms, his feet.

"The *blood* of life, my child," he moans, and begins to massage his hands, arms, legs and feet, drawing the life back to the surface.

"The *breath* of life," Beni' whispers, as he kisses Tim's lips, and embraces him fully. He holds the kiss for several seconds, and then lays him back.

"I call you back from the body of the earth. The earth shall surrender her dead unto me..." His voice trails off as the boy appears at his elbow. The boy in black looks at Timothy for a long time, his soft brown eyes calm, his face beautiful.

"...the earth shall surrender her dead unto me," the youth intones, and Benediction's voice rises and falls with his as the old magic alights the air around them with brilliance.

I am aghast, as is Brian, and Arik is rather startled himself as the ceremony continues.

Who is this boy?

I hear the drums of the dead, the chanting of ritual magic, the spirits of the light and the dark. The voices of both Bocor and Houngon throughout the ages murmur and rustle.

Brian and Arik do not hear these things.

I have learned to listen to the night.

"My child, may our blood become yours, and bring you strength. May you awaken and live once more," Benediction utters, as he puts the chalice near Timothy's lips and wets them with the blood. "*Live* once more," Benediction commands, and kisses his lips. He beckons me to the pulpit, and I gaze down at Timothy's handsome face. His lashes are black and curl softly upon his cheeks, the prominent cheekbones are beautiful, and I feel a stirring deep within me.

"That's *good*," Benediction, sensing my desire, whispers to me. "Now, *take* him, Matty."

I lift Timothy by the shoulders and anoint his lips with the blood from the chalice.

"The *blood* of life."

I kiss his lips very gently.

"The *breath* of life."

I take a breath, and close my eyes. "*Live* once more. I call you back from the body of the earth. The earth shall surrender her dead unto me."

I hold him in my arms, this beautiful child, and my heart aches. It is obvious that he is much loved. I am glad now that I have given him my eternal gift. I just hope that he will not hate me for it.

I kiss him again, and my heart is in it. Brian's eyes meet mine from across the room, and he lowers his head.

Benediction comes up from behind and embraces me. I hear his wings expand, and the two of us, Timothy and I, are completely covered.

Benediction sings once more, but the song is now of a dark, primal quality. I feel Beni' step back from us, and a golden light encases Timothy's body. All of his wounds from the dagger are instantly healed, his hair and body are clean, and his cheeks are losing that sunken look. The light energy quickens around him, but he remains still.

I am seized with a fierce passion, and before I can control it, I kiss his mouth deeply, his throat, his shoulders and chest, his belly. I strive to draw the life back to the surface with my lips, fingertips and tongue.

I can hear Brian sobbing.

I don't care.

I caress his legs, and explore between them gently with my hand. No response at all.

Frustrated, I release him from my embrace and weep. All of the misery and confusion from the last two days finally overwhelms me, and I throw myself across Timothy's supine form. I have failed Brian, this I know for sure, and I can never replace the companion that I have taken from him so savagely.

I can feel my heart breaking...I can feel it being ripped to shreds.

Benediction, still singing, grasps my shoulders, and then turns me around to face him.

'Try again,' he speaks in my mind, behind my psychic wall.

'I can't,' I respond silently. *'I've lost everything.'*

'Have you?' Benediction smiles, inside my head, and I'm startled to find Brian standing beside me.

"Go *on*, Matthias. It's okay," Brian reassures me.

I bend over Timothy once more, and press my mouth over his beautifully sculpted lips. I hold the kiss for an eternity, and then lay him back.

"*Breathe*, damn you," I whisper fiercely, and my tears fall upon his face. Brian watches me, his hand in mine, supporting me silently.

The light energy intensifies, brightens, and there's a gasp from Brian.

Timothy's eyelashes flutter, then he opens his eyes.

"*Tim*???" Brian smiles, his eyes glimmering like prisms. Timothy blinks twice, and then sits up on the altar.

"Brian, what *happened*? How did I get *here*? The last thing I remember is being at home...and you were with that *ghoul*--"

I snarl, and Beni' puts his arm around me reassuringly.

Ghoul, indeed! I am insulted.

"Oh, Timmy, I'm so *sorry*..." Brian embraces him, and Tim leans on him.

"Brian, I feel so *strange*..."

"You were dead for over twenty four hours, my Beautiful One," Benediction informs him. "Here, drink this," he tells Tim, and gives him the chalice. "It will make you strong again." Timothy sips from it, and then grimaces.

"What *is* this?"

Benediction smiles kindly. "Just a little *wine*." The corners of his eyes crinkle up as his smile grows wider. "Go *on*, you'll feel *much* better."

Timothy grasps the chalice with both hands and starts to drink again, and then spots me in the corner with Arik and the boy. "That's *him*! He's the one who, *who*--"

Beni' smiles at him, but the strain of the previous two days is beginning to show.

"Well, you're *alive* now, Son," he says, rather shortly. "Now *drink* it."

Tim hands the chalice to Brian. "I don't *want* it! Who *are* these people? What's *happening?"*

Brian sighs, and catches my eye from across the room. Understanding passes silently between us. He nods. "Drink it for *me*, Timmy?" He flutters his lashes, and gives him a coquettish smile.

Tim rolls his eyes in the way of a reply, and gulps down the blood.

Benediction and I smile at each other, for we both know that the immortal ceremony will not take effect unless the blood is consumed.

My heart is suddenly heavy as I remember yet another stipulation of the immortal ritual. I wonder if it will shatter what Brian and I have between us forever.

Chapter Ten

Benediction takes Timmy by the hand, and stands him before him. Timothy, who certainly has no problem with being naked in the presence of men, stares back at him, bold as can be.

"Red would be nice, I think," Benediction muses, and briefly enfolds him within his wings. As he steps back from Timothy, I can now see why Tim holds such a powerful sway over the men of Orleans. He's clothed in a red peasant shirt with a high neck, tight black leather trousers, and thigh high stiletto boots. His chestnut hair is long and sleek, his skin as pale as marble, his eyes a fiery green, and his lips as red as heart's blood.

"*Wow*," I breathe, impressed. "You're *beautiful*."

"*Am* I?" Timothy teases with a sexy smile, as he sits down, crosses his legs, and begins adjusting a strap at the ankle of his boot.

Completely captivated by this vision before me, I study the slim line of his leg, encased in black leather, and I stifle a moan.

Unfortunately, desire will sometimes not be denied, and my trousers are doing very *little* to hide the fact that I'm enraptured with Timothy.

Tim's clever face is amused, and a wide grin appears. "Oh, is that for *me*?"

I nod weakly.

"*Well*," he smiles, rising from the pew and grasping my belt, "Perhaps we should be going?"

I glance over at Brian, whom, thanks to Beni', is conversing enthusiastically with Arik and the curly haired youth. The boy's hand is on Brian's knee, and I frown, but Beni' is making shooing gestures at me.

The ceremony must be completed.

I offer my arm to the beautiful creature at my side. He takes it in a rather stiff and formal manner, and smiles up at me, lips closed.

We walk in silence for a while, and like any man in love, I notice the differences between my current companion and my beloved. He is a good seven inches shorter than Brian, but he is slender and long limbed, and beautiful as a black lily. Good breeding and fine manners are apparent in his every gesture, very different from my Brian, who is childlike and innocent and rather artless, but in a charming way.

"Champagne?" he asks me, as I remove my jacket and sit down on the couch. I notice a bloodstain from the previous evening, and hurriedly cover it with one of the large, tasseled pillows. Seeing his own blood may frighten him...although he hasn't shown any fear of me since he finished the blood mixture from the chalice and taken my immortal blood into his veins. He is now a vampire, the same as I.

When he returns, I notice that he has removed the trousers and jacket, and is now dressed in a tight, short leather skirt, black stockings, garters, stiletto boots, and a tight, netty, long sleeved black top.

"Champagne?" I reply, momentarily bedazzled by the length of his legs and the blood red shade of his lips. "Oh, yes. *Please.*"

He fills a glass and passes it to me, then pours one for himself. "*So*," he says smoothly, grinning as he seats himself by me, "What exactly do you *do*, when you're not ghooming about, nibbling upon the necks of innocent young men?"

"You are *hardly* innocent, my little cupcake," I tease. He raises his brows, and sips his champagne, then clears his throat.

"Perhaps not." He blushes a bit, as I place my hand on his knee and rub gently. He looks into my eyes, and I am entranced.

I lift his chin and guide his lips to mine.

"Mm. Come *here*." He throws his leg over my hip, and I grasp his buttock hard enough to leave a bruise.

"Mercy," Timothy whispers. "Be gentle with me. I *break*."

I laugh, and pull him on top of me.

"*Come* to me," I plead, as he lays atop me, hands on my chest, hair falling softly down upon my face, our bodies pressed hip to hip.

"I cannot be much closer," he protests, smiling, as I slip my fingers underneath the tops of his stockings. He sits up, straddling my body, and tosses back his magnificent chestnut mane.

"You are incredibly sexy," I tell him, as he begins to undulate sensually, his palms flat on my belly as I grasp his stockinged thighs.

He removes his shirt, throws his head back, smiles, and bites his lip.

"So are *you*," he moans, and puts his finger in his mouth. He climbs off of me so that I can get to my feet and stand before him.

"*Hey*, there," I smile at him, as he begins to unfasten the garters. "Leave the stockings." He complies, unzips the skirt, and slides it off, down the length of his thighs. I sink to my knees, embrace his legs, and rub my face in his smooth, white belly. He is beautiful, fully erect. I kiss one milky white thigh, then the other.

He sighs, his hands in my long, black hair. I gaze up at him, and his hair is lit by the lamp behind him. It looks almost like a halo, but I know that this sweet child has the devil inside of him...or that he soon *will*.

I take him deep within my mouth, and he bites his lip and whimpers.

"You're *incredible*," he moans, as I release him and sit him down on the couch. I take a seat beside Timothy, and guide his hand to my belt.

He colors prettily, smiles, and has me unclothed quickly. My shirt remains, open and loose, but he makes no immediate move to remedy that fact. Instead, he kneels in front of me, moves between my legs, and licks the insides of my thighs.

I groan, my hands in his fine, silky mane, and guide his head to me gently. His mouth is warm and wet, and I find myself struggling to halt the pleasure which is building in my loins, layer upon torturous layer.

Timothy senses that I'm ready, grasps my thighs, and pushes himself up to a standing position. He turns from me, bends at the waist, and makes an adjustment to the seam in his stocking, one leg slightly in front of the other. His body is sleek and smooth, white as alabaster. He flips back his hair and smiles lazily at me, emerald eyes glinting with mischief like a naughty child's.

I go to him, rest my hand on his lower back and caress his smooth, milky, bare buttocks with the other.

He shrieks as I slap his ass, and then laughs.

"*Do* you--?" he grins, and I nod. He reaches into a drawer and produces a jar, which he places in my hand.

Normally, I do *not*, but Timothy will remember this night forever.

He is a virgin of sorts, after all. His first time as an immortal. I want it to be pleasurable for him.

I open the jar and scoop out some of the ointment with two fingers. It has an odor of cinnamon and sugar.

"*Nice,*" I purr, as I gently lubricate him, and then myself. It has a slight tingling sensation which only adds to my desire. I pull him up and back against me, and kiss his neck. He reaches back and touches my face.

"Mm, you're so *tasty*," I murmur, and I lick his ear.

His breath is coming fast, and he's nearing orgasm. I slide my hand down his flat belly, and down to his manhood. I hesitate, and then pull firmly.

"Oh!" he cries, and erupts.

I press his hips back against me, and lay my cheek in his hair. When he is finished, I enter him gradually. He's nice and snug; his beautiful body moves like music with mine. He is sharing my ecstasy; we are connected both physically and telepathically.

When I'm done, I collapse over him on the floor, fully spent. He climbs on top of me, and traces my lips with one fingertip.

"That was *nice*," he smiles. "We'll have to do this again."

[27]

I feel a bit uncomfortable with that, but I have more urgent matters to deal with. He smiles at me.

"What's on your mind, Dear?"

"We have to talk," I tell him gently. "There's something that I must tell you."

He pouts.

"Is this *bad* news?"

"No, to the contrary."

He smiles, and kisses my lips.

"Good."

He and I get to our feet, and move to the couch again.

He sips his champagne, and waits for me to speak.

I stare at him, not knowing where to begin.

"*Timothy*," I say, finally, "There is a certain order to things that *be*." He nods, frowning. "You are my responsibility now, to an extent. I've given you a gift..."

"*Indeed*," he grins, looking down at the two folded one hundred dollar bills that I've slipped into the top of his stocking. "Thank you so much!" He kisses my cheek, and wipes off the lipstick print with his thumb. "I hope that I didn't *disappoint* you?" He pouts, but his eyes are very serious.

I catch his fingers in mine, and cradle his cheek in my hand.

"*Never*," I reassure him warmly. "On the contrary. You were amazing."

"Then...*what*...?"

"You're a *vampire*," I blurt out. "There was a ceremony to raise you from the dead, and I gave you my blood."

He looks perplexed. "I don't *understand*..."

"I know you don't, Cupcake," I reply sadly. "Benediction will be here shortly to explain more. I'm sorry that I did this to you."

Chapter Eleven

I hold Timothy close to me, in these wee hours of the morning. He has leaned on me for hours, playing with my hair, his head upon my chest. He is silent, rather like a child, and has closed in upon himself.

"Tim?" He murmurs wordlessly in response. "Baby, it's time for bed. We need to close the curtains and move into the back room."

He sighs.

"I'm comfortable here."

"It's not safe here, Cupcake. When the sun rises, we should be well protected from the light."

He sighs again, and I gaze up at the clock on the wall. Four fifty-five a.m.

"Come on, let's go," I say briskly, and pat his leg.

"Just hold me, Matty...can you just *hold* me for a second?"

I scoop him up in my arms, and his arms encircle my neck. He looks so weary, so exhausted.

My heart aches for him, and I don't understand how I have become so damned emotional lately. As I lay him on the bed, he looks up at me, his eyes heavy with impending sleep. I smooth back his hair, and he tries to smile.

"Matty?" He looks very sad.

"What is it?"

"I'll never see another sunrise, will I?"

My heart is heavy. "No. Never again."

"I'll never feel the sun on my face, or see a field full of flowers in full bloom."

"*Lots* of flowers bloom at night," I reassure him, and he sighs.

"Bring me flowers every day, Matt...*please*?" He is weeping silently. "*Promise* me."

I, too, am weeping at this point, and I tighten my lips and nod quickly. He sits up in bed, and takes my hands in the two of his.

"Bring me a glass of water, if you please?" I nod again, quite unable to speak, and rise to close the curtains. I fill a glass in the kitchen, and bring it to him. He sips it, and then sets it aside.

"Thank you," he says quietly.

"You're welcome," I smile sadly, my voice husky with tears. He touches my cheek gently, and looks at me for a long time.

"I can see into your heart, Matthias..."

"What do you see?" I ask him, and he looks back at me with his solemn little face.

"You're not telling me *everything*," he frowns.

"Well, what do you want to know?"

His green eyes are boring holes into mine, and I feel his hands against my psychic wall, inside my head. I grab the telepathic link and strengthen it, as I throw the doors to my mind wide open, and invite him in.

~*~*~*~

He is walking beside me in the sacred dark, I cannot see him, but I can feel him grasping my arm. "It's so dark in here," he tells me. "Light a candle, I cannot see." I am silent, but a plethora of candles blaze to life all around us.

Our feet are on a lonely landscape, at the edge of a deep abyss. A thick cloud cover obscures the sky, and the abyss swirls with mist.

"There's something I must know," he tells me, his voice grave. "Why did you kill me? What made you do it? Why me?" he demands suddenly, his voice rising in anger. "Exactly what did I do?"

"It was fate," I tell him simply. "You were in the wrong place at the wrong time."

"Oui...Fate," he sneers. "Well, my good fortune, then."

"I'm so sorry, *Cupcake," I try, but he holds up his hand for silence.*

"Two: what were you doing with Brian?"

"It would have been he who had died if you hadn't interrupted us," I say shortly, and he shakes his head.

"There's more to it than you're telling me."

"I don't know what you mean."

He studies me carefully, reading my emotions, my memories, and lastly, my heart.

"You loved *him?" Tim gasps, and then smiles, and moves closer. "And now you love* me?"

I am surprised myself, but I know that its true...one's greatest desire is not able to deny itself in one's mind. A confusing rush of emotions throbs within me: guilt, bewilderment, discomfort, parental protective instincts...and love. A love so strong and pure that I'm tempted to fall to my knees in front of Timothy and pledge my troth, once and for all. I take his slim hands in mine, and am about to do just that, when he grabs the telepathic link and pulls me into his mind...

~*~*~*~

Behind Tim's psychic wall, the sun is shining, and the barren landscape upon which we were previously standing is lushly green, with flowers of all colors strewn about, and the area is bordered with trees. There is a small waterfall which empties from its rocky wall to the stream below.

"It's beautiful here, Cupcake," I tell him, as he leads me to an old-fashioned ivory colored couch beside the water and hands me a glass of pink champagne. I notice for the first time that he is now clothed in white, from the suede thigh high stiletto boots, to the soft calfskin breeches, to the blousy shirt with the flowing sleeves and the high ribboned neck. He seats himself beside me and smiles.

"This is my special room, where I go when I need to be alone, when I'm sad, or when my body aches, or when I hurt in my heart."

"Are you hurting now?" I ask, as I run my fingers through the silky tangle of his hair, and then touch his face. He leans his cheek upon my hand. "Timothy, you're crying," I say gently. "Talk to me." His beautiful green eyes are very bright.

"It hurt, *you know," he tells me, his voice trembling. "It really hurt when you...ripped my throat out...I-I was terrified...and then the world began to recede in waves, as if in a faint...and I felt s-so* odd...*and suddenly, I was at the church, and Brian was there. I was covered in blood, and that guy in white was standing over me. He wanted me to drink this...wine. I was so frightened...I wanted to run away screaming, I was terrified...and that guy in white--"*

"--Benediction--"

"--Benediction...he practically forces *me to drink it, and I'm glad that he did. It made the fear go away, and the weakness that I felt was gone instantly."*

"Do you know now that you will live forever?"

"Oh, Matty, no *one lives forever."*

"You will. *I gave you my blood in that cup. We all did...Brian, Arik, I, the boy, Beni'--"*

"Who?"

"The guy with the wings."

"The guy in white? The redhead?"

"How many guys do you know with wings?" I tease gently, and he smiles and sniffs, the tears already fading.

"I thought that I had imagined them, that I was hallucinating."

"No, they're very real."

He sighs, and leans on my shoulder. "Matty, hold me."

I take him in my arms again, the two of us basking in the sunshine in this portal of his mind, and my heart is very full.

~*~*~*~

We find ourselves back in the bedroom once more. I light the lamps, and look over at Tim, who is watching me. He certainly looks calmer, but he still looks puzzled. I sit down on the bed, and unzip one of his stilettos.

"Benediction will be here soon to explain more," I tell him, as I remove the other boot, and detach the garters. "We should probably hop in the tub before they get back."

"Your hair needs a good washing, I think," Tim says very matter-of-factly, and I notice that it is, indeed, a bit grimy. Tim pulls off his stockings, and I watch him walk ahead of me into the bathroom.

'Wow, nice haunches,' I think silently, completely forgetting that Timothy, as an immortal, can now read my unguarded thoughts. He turns back and grins at me; I blush, and he takes me by the hand.

~*~*~*~

An hour later, we are sitting at the kitchen table talking when the four of them arrive home. We can hear them talking and laughing from the back of the house, and it's very obvious that they've imbibed.

I'm fervently wishing that Benediction has had the sense to remain sober, but my hopes are completely dashed when he appears in the doorway, his arms around Brian and the boy in black. They are supporting him, propping him up on either side. Beni' is clearly up in the stratosphere for the time being, and Brian and the boy are struggling to keep him on his feet.

It would be a comical sight on any other night but this one. I have been counting on Beni' to explain to Tim in detail the immortal/vampire subject, to help put Tim's mind at ease.

Instead I get *this*.

"Idiot." I clench my teeth. Beni' giggles, and Brian scolds him.

"Be *cool*, man!"

Arik edges around them, nods to me, and plants a kiss on the top of Timothy's head.

"So," he says, pulling up a chair and leaning his chin on the back of it, "How *are* you?"

Tim's face is grave.

"I'm *well*, thank you." Arik reaches over and ruffles his hair, and Tim cries: "Arik! Your *arm!*"

There is a long, raised scar down his forearm. We all have them now. Benediction did heal us earlier, but the scars will remain forever, as a reminder of our devotion to Timothy.

Arik rests his brow against Tim's.

"A *small* price to pay to have you back, my dear friend." They smile at each other.

I roll my eyes at Beni', who has pretty much passed out at this point.

"Put him to bed," I command, and Brian gasps.

[31]

"No! Not on my silken bedcovers! Absolutely *not*!"

"On the *couch*, then," I snarl, irritated. The two of them, Brian and the boy, ease Beni' onto the couch and pull a blanket over him.

"Ugh," Brian grimaces. "He *stinks.*"

"Well, he *did* drink half a pint of Jack Daniels," the boy grins.

"Yes, and he had some absinthe with me, and a couple of beers with Arik," Brian muses.

"He's as drunk as a goddamned *skunk*," Arik affirms, as Benediction begins to snore.

"*Skunk* is definitely the right word." Brian wrinkles his nose. "Wow, what a *stench!*"

"Give him a break," the boy smiles. "It's been a long night."

Arik kisses Tim's cheek gently, and whispers in his ear. Tim closes his eyes and shakes his head.

"Well, it *has* been a rather odd evening," Arik smiles, his arm loosely around Tim's shoulders. "Are you going to bed soon?"

"*Non*, I don't feel like making love tonight, Arik. I'm sorry. Don't be mad."

Arik looks a bit sad, but replies:

"*Soon*, then."

Not if I can help it.

I cross over to Arik and Timothy, and am surprised by the look in Tim's eyes. It's a look that I've seen many times in my own...

"Arik, you need to take Brian and the boy out of here--quickly!"

Arik frowns at me.

"There's no need to be *thorny*, Matthias. I'll keep my hands to myself tonight--"

"GET *OUT*!" I cry. "Don't argue!"

"Matty," Tim groans. "Matty, what's *happening* to me?"

"OH...MY...*GOD!!!*" Brian gasps. "Timmy, your *teeth--!*"

Tim's fangs have cut through.

"Arik, get them *out* of here!!!" I plead. "Go *on!* MOVE!!!!"

Brian continues to stare, but Arik moves away from Tim quickly and catches Brian by the arm.

"Let's *go!*"

The boy immediately follows suit.

"Come *on*, Brian...stop gawking, and let's *go!*" The three of them leave, the boy and Arik pulling Brian along, who keeps looking back over his shoulder at Tim. The scent of jasmine is heavy in the air.

When the door is safely closed, and the light from outside is effectively blocked, I turn back to Timothy.

"Oh, Cupcake..." He looks frightened.

"Matty, I feel faint," he moans. "I'm so *dizzy...*"

I reach behind me for a knife from the drawer.

I flip my hair to one side, and make a small incision over the side of my throat.

He watches me, a grim look of foreboding on his face.

I pull back his hair and administer the same wound to his neck.

The blood spurts at first, and then trails down our pale skins.

I dab some of my own blood on my fingertips and anoint his mouth with it.

He licks his lips, and his gaze meets mine. The green in his eyes has a luminous quality, as if it's being lit from within. There is also a feral cruelty present. He begins to pant, and he is suddenly in my arms, his head tucked under my chin, his warm, wet little mouth pressed to my throat.

Mm, I'm so hard I goddamn fucking *ache*.

He moves into my lap, and I press him close. I find the wound in his throat with my lips, and I groan with pleasure. Timothy is enraptured as well.

Good blood is sweeter than sex.

I grasp his buttocks as he straddles me; he wraps his legs around my waist. I explore his legs with my fingers and hands, then slip one hand between them. He cries out, his face in my hair, his manhood pushing against my belly as I stroke him gently.

"Matty," he moans, as I rest my cheek against his long, soft hair, and he presses my head to his chest with the palm of his hand. "Matty..."

"What is it, Cupcake?" I whisper, as he untangles my hair with his fingers, and sighs from deep within his chest. "Timothy, what?"

He leans his cheek against the top of my head and sighs again.

"Matty--...*Matthias, I-I...*"

I raise my head to look at him, but he presses my head to his heart once more.

"Thank you for...*choosing* me," he says very seriously, his hand stroking my hair gently.

What an odd thing to say! I close my eyes, and listen to his chest: the beating of his heart, the soft stirring of his breath, the sound of his voice. There is nowhere that I'd rather be at the moment.

"*How* could I choose anyone else?" I reply, and although I cannot see his face, I know that he is smiling.

"I *love* you," he says, his voice still very serious. I smile against the warmth of his silken hair, and breathe in his scent. His heart is beating rapidly as he awaits my reply, and I am suddenly and very solemnly aware that, two days ago, I stilled his heart myself, without any thought or hesitation. The passage from his previous life was painful, bloody and horrific...and his reentry into the world of the living was much the same, full of fear and confusion.

Yet, this dear child tells me that he *loves* me.

I move his hair aside, and kiss the flesh of his chest, over his heart. I feel it stir beneath my lips, and realize how each heartbeat is precious, and that it is now eternal.

He is an immortal. We are now equally yoked.

"I love you, *too*," I tell him, and raise my head to look at him. He is teary eyed, his lips trembling.

"*Matty...*" He smiles through his tears at me, and laughs.

"Give me your hand," I smile, and place a platinum, cut diamond band on his finger. It is a beautiful ring, very slim and finely etched, much like the hand on which it now resides.

"I *love* it," he smiles, and the two of us gaze at each other for an eternity before our lips meet in a tender kiss.

Chapter Twelve

"You are the most beautiful vampire I've ever seen," I tell my new husband, as he clasps his hands together and rests his chin on them atop my chest. His silken hair is unbound, and falls in thick, shining waves around his face and shoulders. He smiles dreamily, and closes his eyes.

"My beloved," he sighs, his smile soft and warm. "I am so happy."

"Me too, Cupcake," I grin, and tuck a stray wisp of his hair behind his ear. "So, where do you want to go on our honeymoon?" I ask him, and he giggles.

"Nowhere. I'm happy here, as long as I'm with you, and as long as I'm yours...and you're mine..."

I kiss the tips of my fingers, and press them to his brow.

"Always," I reassure him, and he smiles in that odd little closed-mouthed way of his which is so endearing.

"*Always*...what a beautiful word."

"Do you want a ceremony?" I ask him quite seriously. He ponders it for a moment, his lips pressed together, and shakes his head.

"Mm-mm. Not now."

I gaze into his serious green eyes, and touch his cheek.

"Why the somber face, Cupcake?"

He sighs. "Haven't you noticed how hard that Brian is taking this?"

I remain silent, but the truth is, yes I have. All day, Brian has been trying to catch my attention, but I've just turned away. Benediction, thankfully, has sobered up enough to intervene so that Timothy and I have a few moments together without interruption.

I pull Timothy on top of me, peck his lips, and then rise and begin to dress.

"The sooner that this problem is dealt with, the better," Tim states rather blatantly, as he brushes out his glorious chestnut mane before the mirror at the dressing table. He smiles as I kiss the top of his head, and then a desolate look sweeps over his face. I take him by the shoulders and kiss his cheek from behind.

"Cupcake?"

His eyes are bright with tears, and his lips are trembling.

"Sweetheart, what's wrong?"

"If you want to go to him--" He bows his head and sobs. My own heart feels as if it's being ripped to shreds, along with his.

"No, no," I soothe, taking the brush from him and setting it aside, before embracing him fully. "*You* are the one that I love. *Always*." I kiss his head again. "Don't cry," I beg, my own voice beginning to tremble. "I choose *you*. It's *always* been you. Since the resurrection."

He sighs.

"You've never told me exactly what happened."

I lead him again to the bed, sit, and draw him down on my knee. He puts an arm around my neck and leans on me.

"Where shall I begin? Benediction and I were arguing over whether to resurrect you or not. I said yes, but he didn't think that it was a good idea. Brian and I were together, but I thought that it would make him happy--"

"Does he *look* happy?" Tim interrupts, his voice weary. I give him a gentle squeeze around the waist and pat his leg.

"Let me *finish*, Cupcake, okay? He missed you so, although he tried to hide it. Your death shook him terribly. Benediction had previously stated to Brian that he couldn't create life where there was no life present, but he lied...he lied for me. He thought that bringing you back to this world would cause Brian to abandon me--"

"It's quite the *opposite* though, isn't it?" His voice has that same weary quality. "Matty, I used to think that Brian was incapable of loving anyone. I loved him myself...as a beggar would love a king. I mean, just *look* at him--"

"--And look at *you*," I smile, as we gaze at our reflection in the mirror. "See *that*?" I grasp his chin in my fingertips and force him to look at himself. "You are so *beautiful*..."

His tears come freely.

"Not like Brian."

"No, I suppose not," I smile tenderly. "But you're *not* Brian, you're *Timothy*..." I turn his cheek to mine, and I gaze at his somber little face "...and you are *exactly* what I've always wanted." He weeps, and I rub his back. "*Shhhh*, hey now," I soothe. "It's okay...Now, where was I...oh, yes. Benediction decided that he was going to get back at me because he was angry at me, and he told Brian the truth about what he could do to bring back your life. Brian was overjoyed. Beni also saved Arik from Obadiah, but he couldn't save Noah...and..."

"OBADIAH???" Tim cries, and begins to tremble.

"He can't hurt you anymore," I remind him, but his body is quaking, and he is pushing against me so close that we're almost wearing the same skin. "Timothy, stop!" I shout very suddenly, and I can feel that he's hiding something from me. He looks at me, but he looks ashamed, afraid...

I reach out in my mind to his, and rest my palms against his psychic wall...

~*~*~*~

'Open up, come on, Cupcake. I can't help otherwise.'

I feel his fear, his sadness, his hesitation, his hopelessness. Physically, it is like a net which catches in my fingers.

'Baby, let me in!' I plead silently.

'No...I'm afraid.'

I can hear him weeping, but he is trapped behind the wall.

'Timothy, I love you,' *I plead, and then I remember something that Benediction once told me:*

'Perfect love conquers all...and casts out all fear.'

The wall crumbles, and I step through the dust and debris to the other side.

I see Timothy, but he is much younger, perhaps thirteen or fourteen, no more. He is on his knees in the rubble, pleading and crying with a tall youth of about twenty with long, flowing, fair hair. The blond pulls him into his arms and rocks him back and forth.

'I'm here, now,' *he says, and they sit among the ruins for hours.* 'What happened with your Dad?' *the blond asks Tim, and Tim cries.*

'He's dead. The sickness took him last night.'

'We'll need to bury him,' *the blond says, and the two of them do just that, as I watch, a silent observer. The blond and Timothy stand beside the grave, and the blond begins to pray to 'IT'. Tim weeps, but he does not add his voice to the prayer. He is wary of any deity who would leave him to fend for himself at such a tender age.*

'So, what will you do now?' *the blond inquires, and Timothy shakes his head.*

'I don't know, Obadiah. My Dad was all that was left.'

OBADIAH???

When the blond turns his head, I see that it is indeed Obadiah, the Obadiah who killed Noah, and nearly killed Arik.

I snarl, and throw myself upon him, but this is only a psychic manifestation of that person, and my hands close upon the empty air. I reach for Tim, but my hand passes right through him.

"I'm here," *Timothy says from behind me, and he is MY Timothy. He takes my arm, and we stand silently together as Obadiah's and the younger Timothy's lives play out before us.*

'Come with me,' *Obadiah smiles.* 'I have a place of my own, and you can stay with me.'

Months pass, and one evening, as Timothy watches Obadiah getting ready for work, he begs for Obadiah to teach him how to do what he does for a living. At this point, it must be noted that Tim is still very innocent. He has been told that Obadiah is an escort, nothing more.

'You're awfully young,' *Obadiah tells him, as he puts down the makeup brush and studies Timothy objectively.* 'You're very beautiful, though. Those eyes...'

Timothy blushes, and looks at his feet, then up at Obadiah again.

'Yes! Do that again! It's great!'

[35]

Tim giggles, and Obadiah smiles.

'They're going to love you!'

'Who?'

'The men of Orleans, silly. Now strip naked and get in the bath. You can come out with me tonight.'

Timothy complies, and Obadiah begins wiping down his back and shoulders with a sponge.

'So what's it like?' *Timothy asks, as he washes his own face with a cloth, then stands so that Obadiah can sponge off his legs, feet and lower back.*

'Well,' *Obadiah replies, his face taking on an odd, dreamlike quality,* 'It's a bit...uncomfortable at first--grab onto me--' *he begins to sponge off his genitals and buttocks* 'Yes, it's a bit uncomfortable at first, but it feels nice after a while...'

Tim grasps Obadiah's shoulder and leans on him for balance, and Obadiah smiles a bit.

'All right, wash your hair, and we'll get you dressed.'

When Tim comes out of the bath, Obadiah goes to him and kisses him hard. Tim pulls away, but Obadiah won't release him.

'Don't look so pained, you little idiot! The clients won't like it. Now, open your mouth, and relax a little.'

Timothy, who is used to being treated kindly by Obadiah, is terrified, and tries to obey, but his body is trembling. Obadiah kisses him again, and Tim presses his palms flat against Obadiah's chest, but doesn't push him away.

'Use your tongue a little more, like I do,' *Obadiah tells him, his voice gentler than before. Tim does as he's told, and soon, they're both enraptured.*

Obadiah finally releases his lips, and begins to kiss his ears, his throat, his shoulders, his chest, his hipbones. His fingers undrape the towel, and Tim's first instinct is to cover himself with his hands.

'No,' *Obadiah tells him, smiling.* 'Just close your eyes and enjoy this.' *He takes Timothy's hands in his, and gently moves them away.*

'No, don't!' *Timothy cries, and Obadiah glares at him.*

'Stop it, you little Shit,' *he growls at him.* 'I'm just trying to prepare you. Don't even THINK about pulling this kind of shit in front of a customer, you HEAR me?'

Timothy begins to cry, but he doesn't make a sound. He looks up at the ceiling, unblinking.

Obadiah takes him in his mouth.

The tears stream down his face, but he clenches his teeth, determined not to provoke Obadiah further.

I look over at my Timothy, who will not meet my eyes.

He is crying, too.

So am I.

I put my arms around him and press him close.

'Let's go,' *I beg him, but now that it's started, the memory must run its full cycle.*

Obadiah finalizes the evening with a brutal act of penetration, and a scream tears itself from Timothy's throat. The scream is deafening, my head throbs with pain, and Tim is cowering in my arms, sobbing hysterically.

~*~*~*~

The psychic link shatters, and we are in the bedroom once more. Benediction is with us; a piece of the doorframe is hanging from the chain lock, where Beni' and Arik have kicked in the door.

"I heard the screaming! What in the *fuck* is going on in here?!!" Benediction shouts at me, his eyes blazing as Arik kneels beside Timothy and tries to soothe him.

[36]

"It-it's horrible," I shudder. "Obadiah--"

At the mention of his name, Timothy screams again, and claws at Arik.

"Don't *touch* me!!!"

Arik backs away, the shock and hurt apparent on his face.

"All right," he says quietly, and sits in a chair by the bed.

"Timothy showed me one of his memories about...Obadi--that blond guy in the white robe. He...raped him when he was thirteen."

"Because I deserved it," Tim moans. "I was always teasing him, making him love me..."

Beni' sighs, and sits down beside him.

"You're a good-looking boy, it's true. But what he did to you was unforgiveable. It was rape. It didn't have anything to do with love."

"But I loved it," Tim cries. "The kissing part, at least..."

Benediction puts his arm around him, and Timothy collapses against him.

"My child, there is nothing wrong with that...the body will react to physical stimulation. It may have been emotional as well...you were quite alone in the world, and he became everything to you all at once...a parent, a friend...and eventually..."

"Oui, I loved him...and he was right...I did grow to love it...when he was nice to me." He hides his face in Benediction's chest and sobs anew. "But he rarely was, and--"

"Oh, my *heart!*" I cry, clutching my chest. "Timothy, please stop...I'm going to be sick...I can't *stand* this..."

"Pull yourself together, Matty," Benediction frowns. "How do you think that *he* feels?"

"Shut up, Beni'," I mutter, as I take Timothy's hand between the two of mine and try to reach him. "Cupcake, listen to me. He hurt you. It wasn't your fault. You were so innocent--"

"No, I wasn't. Look at me, Matty! I became exactly what he said that I was!"

"So you're a prostitute! So fucking *what!* There's nothing wrong with that!" I shout at him.

"Oui...but I repeated the cycle, don't you see? With Brian? That makes *me* a monster too..."

"No," Brian says softly, from the doorway. "It wasn't like that with us. I was older, I was almost seventeen...and I---I wanted it. I wasn't afraid...you were so gentle and sweet with me."

Timothy holds out his hand, and Brian crosses the room to take it in his.

"I've never really thanked you for all that you've done for me. I know that I'm silly, and vain, and completely selfish, but I do love you, after a fashion."

Timothy stares at Brian, and smirks.

"You know, that's the nicest, most straightforward thing that you've ever said to me..."

I look at Benediction, who is biting his lip and trying not to laugh. I shift my gaze to Arik, who is looking at Brian incredulously.

"You're really a piece of work, you know that? How did this become all about *you?"*

"I was simply trying to make him feel better--"

"*No*, what you're *trying* to do is make Matty jealous by cozying up to Timothy! Why? It's not like you ever *cared* about Tim before!"

"*ARIK!!!*" Benediction's voice is like thunder.

"No, Beni', I have to say this! If you *truly* love Timothy, and if you love Matty, you'll leave them the fuck alone and let them be happy! Stop moping around here like a two year old child! Get out of bed, take a bath, wash your hair, and go back to work!"

Brian starts to tear up, and Arik shouts:

[37]

"Don't try to pull that shit with me! I know *exactly* what you are...what *drives* you. You can roll those big brown eyes at Beni', or Matty to get your way, but it won't work with *me*, you whore!" He pushes past Brian and storms out of the room.

We are all silent, because as harsh as those words are, there is much truth in them. I do hurt for Brian, and I feel that I owe him something, a small gesture. I rub his back, and tell everyone, "That's not *entirely* true...Timothy, Brian cried when you died, and when we buried you, he became hysterical. He *loves* you, Tim."

Tim squeezes Brian's hand. "I *know* you do," he says warmly.

There is a loud crash, then another. Arik is punching the wall, swearing.

Benediction kisses Timothy's cheek. "Are you okay now?" he asks tenderly.

"Mm-hm," Tim replies, and there's another crash, followed by the sound of breaking glass.

"I'd best go to him," Beni' states, and leaves the room.

"I'll go too," Brian says quietly, and leaves Timothy and I alone again.

"Well?" Timothy says very suddenly. I jump.

"Well, what?"

"Aren't you going to go after Brian? He's pretty upset."

"Cupcake!" I exclaim. "*You* are the one I love. Remember what I said earlier? I will love you, *always."*

"Even now?" he asks, his face very solemn.

"Of course."

He smiles.

"You really *mean* it, don't you?"

"I *do*," I affirm, kissing the ring on his hand. He grabs me by the lapels of my jacket and pulls me down on top of him on the bed. "Hey, I almost forgot...I brought you something," I smile, and he tugs at my belt.

"Is it *big*?"

I laugh.

"Yes, Sweetheart, that *too,"* I tease, and I reach into my jacket.

"Oh, Matt! I love it!" he smiles, as I give him one perfect, long stemmed white rose. "You kept your promise to me!"

I peck his lips.

"Flowers every day. That's the deal."

He laughs. It bubbles up from within him like champagne on crystal. He is so beautiful when he is happy, his alabaster skin, his eyes as bright as two stars, his hair shining like the sea, and his lips and cheeks like the soft pink petals of a rose.

"What precisely are you *staring* at?" he smiles, as I gaze down on him and touch his face.

"You," I answer truthfully.

"Well, *why?"*

"Because you're *there*, you silly ass," I tease him. "Why else?"

A smile tugs at the corners of his mouth. "You're very *odd."*

I kiss one corner of his mouth, then the other.

"Ee-yup."

He frowns.

"Don't say *yup*, it makes you sound simple."

"Uhhhmm...h'okay."

"Matty!!!" he laughs.

"Duh?"

He cracks up completely.

"You're certifiable!"

"Doy!"

"Matthias, *stop!"* he chortles, "I'm *serious!* I'm going to *barf!"*

"I *love* your barf, My Darling!" I make an odd face at him, and bury my face in his neck. He shrieks with laughter, tears streaming down his face and into his hair.

"Get *off* of me!" he chuckles. "It's almost nightfall."

"Let's stay in tonight," I murmur against his throat. He rests his hands in my hair for a second, then pulls.

"Ow!" I yelp.

"I have to *work*, Matty. Bring me some champagne, if you please."

"Only if you'll miss me when I'm gone."

He studies his nails. "I'll *manage*, Matthias...I'm fine."

"You sure *are*," I leer at him.

He throws a pillow at me as I'm leaving. It strikes me square in the butt, and I pause for a moment, muttering under my breath. Tim giggles and covers his mouth, his eyes sparkling with mischief, like a naughty child's.

"Oh," I frown, feigning disgust. "Oh, shit, are you going to *get* it!" I grin, and leap on him, pillow in hand.

"Ow! Mercy!" he yelps, as I start smacking him with the huge feather pillow about the shoulders and face. "No fair! There's no other pillow!"

"You should have thought about that *before*!" I gloat, and launch an all-out attack on his body and legs, with Tim tugging at the other end of the pillow, trying to regain possession of the solitary weapon with which he's being mercilessly pummeled.

"Stop, I can't breathe!" he shrieks with laughter, and falls on his back. "I surrender!"

"We-e-elllll...okay," I tease, "Just as long as you acknowledge who's the *man* around here!"

He thinks about it for a moment, and smirks.

"Okay..."

I grin triumphantly.

"...keep *hitting* me, then."

The smile drops off my face, and transfers to his. He beams at me, all teeth.

"Why, you *brat!"* I gasp in mock annoyance.

He pouts.

"Where's my champagne, *Goofball?"*

"Coming right up, *Barf Bag,"* I grin, and we both completely lose it again.

Benediction knocks on what's left of the bedroom door, but he's discreetly turned his back.

"We're heading out soon, in about twenty minutes, if you want to come with."

Tim and I are practically spitting on each other to keep from collapsing into another fit of laughter.

"No," I groan through my nose, my voice cracking with the effort. "We'll go out later." Tim is cramming his fists in his mouth, chortling and kicking his feet, trying to keep the laughter in. He's not doing so well. I grin at him, and turn back to Beni', who is still looking away. "See you later, huh?"

Beni' raises his hand and waves.

[39]

"Sure thing...*Barf Bag.*"

Tim falls on the floor, rolling and shrieking. I do my best to close the door, and then take a seat beside him.

"Hey, *I'm* Goofball, and *you're* Barf Bag," I mutter, and Tim starts coughing, trying to catch his breath, slowly becoming more like himself again.

"Oh, that was so *funny,*" he gasps. "I haven't laughed like that since I was a small child."

"It's good for you, Cupcake," I smile. "You should do it more often."

"We don't have time tonight. I have to get ready."

He leaves to take a shower, and I go into the front room. Brian is drinking a glass of wine, and Arik is leaning back against the wall, looking sulky.

"Hey," I say to Arik, who nods, and then touch Brian's hair.

He has taken Arik's advice, and is in full regalia and ready for work. He has used a lot of cologne, but I can still smell the jasmine of his misery. He is in extreme emotional pain, but trying desperately to hide it.

"Brian, thank you for what you said in there. It meant the world to Timothy."

His lips pull down at the corners, and he nods.

When he doesn't reply, I turn to leave.

"Thank you for standing up for me. I *do* love Tim, just not in that way."

I touch his cheek.

"I know that, Darling, and Tim knows that too."

He leans his cheek on my hand, and manages a sad smile.

"Are you *happy*, Matthias? With Tim?"

I smile back.

"Gloriously so."

"Then I'll do my best to be happy for you...but it's going to be hard to let you go."

Arik watches us, an odd look on his face. I catch his eye, and he arches an eyebrow at me and smirks.

Chapter Thirteen

"Benediction has never looked more beautiful," the youth says admiringly, as we watch Tim and Arik apply his coral-tinted blush and line his beautiful eyes in a smoky black.

"He's a good looking man, all right," I affirm.

"Your Timothy can work magic with a makeup brush," the youth grins. I turn to him and smile.

"I like your new look. You're like a different person--" He looks hurt, and I hurriedly add "--but you look *so* much better. You're the only guy I know who can rock a dress and combat boots."

"I like what he did with my hair," he grins. "It's much easier to care for."

"Dreadlocks," I smile. "On *you*, they look great."

Tim strolls over, Arik in tow, and fixes the boy with an objective look.

"Your turn," he frowns, and grasps the boy's chin between his finger and thumb. "Arik, what do you think?"

"Well, his eyes and lips are his best features, so perhaps a red shade on the mouth, and golden brown on his lids..."

The youth patiently waits while Tim and Arik fuss over him, and slowly, an old-fashioned, Hollywood-style beauty begins to emerge from his solemn features.

They first apply a flesh-colored base to even out his beautiful skin, then brush over it with a mousse-to-matte shade in the palest alabaster pink. Arik lines the boy's full, sensual lips with a deep brick-hued pencil and smudges the line gently with his thumb, before applying a matte cream lipstick with a small brush. He takes a pot of similarly hued powder blush and applies it to his cheekbones and over his lovely high brow, then dusts the upper part of his cheekbones with a shimmery white powder. "To make your cheekbones more prominent," Arik explains.

Tim begins to work on his beautiful eyes, first dusting the entire lid with a golden brown, then filling in the lid crease with black shadow, and highlighting his brow bones with a shimmering gold. He fills in his brows with a brown pencil, lines the entire eye in matte black, blending upwards, and then applies jet black mascara. "Almost done," Tim smiles at him, then says to Arik, "Hand me that gold pencil...and make sure it's sharp..." He cocks his head, and works quickly, highlighting the cupid's bow of the boy's lip with gold, and smudging the center of the bottom lip to create the illusion of fullness. Not that he needs it. His mouth is full and ripe-looking, and his large, dark eyes look deep and smoldering under his long, thick lashes.

"Beautiful," I smile at Tim. "You're a genius, Cupcake." I peck his cheek.

"Well, I had a good canvas, didn't I, Jesse?"

"Jesse? So that's your name?"

Jesse gives me a rather bored look.

"Ummmm...*yeah--?"*

"Well, you never *told* us," I grin, a bit irritated by his attitude. He unwraps a lollipop, shoves it into his mouth, and then shoots me a baleful look.

"You never *asked."* He kisses Tim's cheek with an audible smack, pats his behind, hops down from the makeup chair, and stalks away without a backward glance. Tim stares after him, shocked into silence.

"There's something about that kid I don't like," I frown, and I glance at Tim, who is studying Jesse's retreating form, with his cheek resting on his hand.

"He *really* needs to learn how to walk in a dress. He's a bit bowlegged."

"TIM!" I exclaim, secretly elated, and he gestures towards Jesse, arms out.

"WELL???!!!!"

"Okay, he's a *bit* artless--"

Tim's brows disappear under his hairline. "Oh *come* now...he makes Brian look like the King of England!"

"CUPCAKE!!!"

"Clomp, clomp, clomp," Tim intones, imitating Jesse's rather heavy footed walk.

"It's the boots, and he's still growing," I tell him, trying not to smile. Tim wrinkles his pert little nose.

"Clod," he spits. I bite my lip and clear my throat.

"He'll mature," I smirk, and jump into the chair. Timothy begins to yank a comb through my long black hair.

"Not if I can bloody help it!!!"

"*Ow*! Cupcake!"

He hugs my neck.

"Sorry, Matty." He kisses my cheek, and we both glance across the room as Brian comes in, stretching and yawning. "'Afternoon," Tim says politely. Brian nods, and perches in the chair beside us. Tim and I look at each other, and then at Arik, who is watching Brian carefully.

I don't know why Arik is so openly hostile, but I aim to find out.

"Excuse me, Cupcake," I say to Tim, and Brian takes my place in the chair and lets Tim fuss over him. "Arik," I smile. "I need your help."

He gives me a funny sort of half-smile.

"Matty, I'm not in the mood for games. Just say what you mean."

"Let's go into the back room, its quieter there."

Tim is staring at me. I blow him a kiss, and he smirks.

"Come on," I say to Arik, and rest my hand on his lower back. "We need to talk."

I notice that now, both Tim *and* Brian are staring at me. They both look upset.

Oh shit.

"Come *on,*" I say, more urgently, and we walk to the bedroom. Once there, I close the door and turn to face Arik, who has removed his jacket, and is now lighting a cigarette. He takes a long drag, and blows out the smoke, his blue eyes smoldering.

"This is a *surprise,*" he smiles, the cigarette dangling from his lips. "It's been a long time, Matt."

I'm drawn to him, but I love Tim too much to risk it.

"I'm sorry, Arik, you misunderstand me. I wanted to talk to you about Brian."

He rolls his eyes wearily and nods.

"*Ja*...so, talk..."

"We all know that Brian can be--"

"Selfish? Thoughtless? *Conceited?*"

"--a bit *difficult* to handle at times. He's rather childlike, and he doesn't always think things through--"

Arik snorts with contempt, and takes another drag.

"He really has you snowed, doesn't he?"

I frown. "What do you mean by that?"

"Ask your Tim," Arik glowers. "He'll tell you all about Brian."

"I want *your* view, Arik." I sit beside him on the bed. "Come *on*, Man. What's going on?"

He looks at his feet, and blows out a cloud of smoke.

"Matt, there are so many people like Brian in our line of work. They can sense what people are looking for...their desires, you know? Well, in our profession, it's a great gift to possess. Unfortunately, it's not a great quality in one's everyday life. It can be used to manipulate others, to use them. If you are a person with a good sense of other people's boundaries, there's no problem...but no one can ever do enough for Brian. He demands a person's full

[42]

attention, their every waking thought. In return, he'll be whatever you want him to be. He knows that you love innocence in a person, so he acts like a little child around you. He knows that you like to feel needed, so he acts helpless. He's not helpless, Matt. He's just *not.* He's very good at getting what he wants. Ask your Tim."

"Benediction told me a little about Brian's background, but not a lot about Tim and Brian's relationship."

Arik utters a derisive laugh.

"*Relationship?* Oh, please...Timothy took him in out of the goodness of his heart. He gave Brian everything he had, including his love. He was very protective of him, very fatherly. Brian wasn't always beautiful. Tim had a lot to do with that. He taught him how to dress, how to style his hair and how to carry himself."

"He did a great job."

"*Ja.* Indeed." Arik lights another cigarette, and I frown.

"Those are really *bad* for you."

He grins.

"Shut *up!* You thought that it was hot two weeks ago. Remember in the rain?"

We smile at each other, and I sigh.

"That seems so long ago." We both close our eyes, and I hug Arik with one arm.

"It was so cold that day, and I'd forgotten my coat--"

"--And I gave you mine," I smile. "You were shivering and sneezing, and trying to look tough--"

"*Macho.*"

I laugh.

"*Macho.* I *hate* that word." We both chuckle, and Arik turns his head to look at me. His blue eyes are warm, and his hand covers mine.

"You covered my shoulders with your coat, and put your umbrella over me, and I lit a cigarette--"

"--And I told you that the umbrella wasn't equipped with a *flue*--"

"You're so *weird*, Matty..." His voice is deeper, and he's leaning towards me. Before I know it, his lips are on mine, and I'm kissing him back.

"No," I say suddenly. "I'm *married*, Arik!"

He looks at me incredulously. "You're *what?*"

"I'm in love with Timothy."

"Well, so am *I!*" he shouts. "*Okay?*"

I sigh. Of *course*. Tim and Arik have always been close. How could I have been so blind? It shows in Arik's every gesture towards Tim. His eyes follow Tim like indentured servants, and caress him lovingly.

I understand the feeling. Timothy is very beautiful...well, no, he isn't perfect: the nose and cheekbones are a bit broad and flat, the chin too short, the eyes deeply set, and there are creases in the corners of his eyes and mouth, but the imperfections are endearing, and add character to his face. He has an impish, appealing look, and catlike green eyes which smolder when he's enamored, and sparkle when he's happy...

"Matty, are you even *listening* to me?"

I snap out of my reverie and take Arik's hand. "Of course, Man. I know that you love him...we all do," I say, trying to duck the issue. Brian's depression is already lying heavily on my heart. How many people do I have to hurt in this circle of my dearest friends? And since *when* do I care about people at all? They're fucking useless, like sheep...no, that's not entirely true. I love my friends. I care about them very much. My heart hurts for both Arik and Brian now. I know that Tim feels badly as well. What can we do? We love each other and cannot bear to be apart for very long. Already, I miss the warmth in his eyes, his smile, the softness of his skin, the perfume of his hair...

"Matty...I've loved Tim for years. We've...*been* with each other, and he was always exactly what I've wanted. You know what I mean?" Arik's eyes plead with mine. "*Release* him, Matty. Give him back to me. *Please?*"

[43]

I sigh, and ruffle his spiky hair.

"I'm sorry, Arik, but I cannot."

He struggles to his feet and grasps blindly for his jacket.

"Arik--"

"Not *now,*" he says quickly, and leaves the room.

I go after him, and run head on into Jesse, who looks after Arik, then glares at me.

"You *dog,*" he snarls.

I resist the urge to shake him violently, and to snap his neck, and instead, push past him.

"Arik, *wait!*" I yell, but he's already headed for the front door. Beni' stops me with one hand against my chest, and I shrink back into the shadows to avoid the daylight and its fire.

"Wait *here,*" Beni' orders me. I open my mouth to cut him off, and he jabs his finger at me. "*BUH! Quiet!* Let me close the door first." He walks across the floor with long, graceful strides, and shuts the door tightly, then comes back to me and embraces me, immediately sensing the torment in my mind and heart. "My Child," he soothes, as I begin to sob. "My *Darling...*"

"Oh, *Beni'!*" I wail. "What do I *do?*"

"Give Arik back to Obadiah," Jesse smirks from the doorway. "Problem *solved*, right?"

Benediction and I both stare at him in shocked silence. Jesse leans on the doorframe and crosses his arms, staring back at us.

"Please *leave* us," Benediction says softly, and Jesse snickers.

"Lucifer, are you still trying to pass yourself off as an angel of *God?*"

"*LEAVE!!!* Right *now!!!*" Benediction thunders. "This is neither the time, nor the place."

"I think it *is,*" Jesse grins. "You are an evil force in the world, and you have driven mankind away from the salvation of my Father's grace."

"*GRACE???*" Benediction thunders. "Your own father created a flawed race like mankind, blamed them for those flaws, killed millions of people at his whim, and as a final coup de grace, nailed his own *Son* to a cross like a side of beef?! Do you call that *grace??? STUPID* CHILD!!!" He seizes Jesse's hands, and holds them in front of his face. "You wear *gloves*, but I *know* who you are! I remember when they crucified you...and afterwards, when you returned to heaven, your loving *Father* cut off your wings!!! You awakened in *my* domain, as I recall...and you *begged* for the fire...but I *healed* you...I had *mercy* upon you...more than 'IT' had for 'IT''s own Son..." Benediction's voice breaks, and he begins to cry. "Jesse, My Child, I *love* you. I am more of a father than 'IT' ever was to you..."

"You're *cursed,*" Jesse glowers at him, and Benediction trembles. I hold him tightly, soothing him, stroking his shoulders and back.

"Beni', don't let him hurt you so--"

But Benediction is trembling with rage, not sadness...

He is shaking with anger.

"Matty, *leave* us," he growls.

"But Beni'--"

"*Now*, Matthias. I have matters to attend to."

Reluctantly, I turn and leave...

Chapter Fourteen

I walk back to the makeup room, where Brian and Tim are sitting in the chairs, chatting. Tim sees my shocked expression, and jumps up in alarm.

"Matty, what's *wrong?"* he panics, and grabs my hands in the two of his. I look at him, my eyes dull, my jaw agape, and he releases my fingers and takes my face in his hands. "Matty, *talk* to me!" Brian embraces me from behind without a word.

We can hear Benediction and Jesse screaming at each other, and the venom of their words tears into my heart like a knife. We all love Beni' like a brother, a father, a lover, a friend. He is the glue which holds us together.

"This Jesse, who *is* he?" Tim cries, as the wall jolts, sending plates and glasses crashing to the floor in the kitchen.

"The son of 'IT'," Brian says quietly. I turn to face him.

"You *knew?"*

He shrugs.

"Of course."

"Why didn't you tell us?" Tim gasps, and Brian's mouth pulls down at the corners.

"You never *asked,"* he replies glibly, smirking.

I slap his face. Hard. Brian tears up, and for once, I feel no pity.

I give him a withering look, and cut him dead.

He walks across the room and stands against the doorway, arms crossed, his back to us.

I pull Timothy close to me, and nestle my face in his hair.

"Oh, Cupcake, I love you so..."

"I love you too, Matty," he says worriedly. "Come, let's lay down. You look exhausted."

Tim puts his arm around my waist, and I sink against him as we start toward the doorway...and we stop dead.

Benediction is standing in the hallway, holding Jesse in his arms. There is much blood everywhere. Jesse and Beni' are covered in it, and Beni' is fading fast.

His eyes terrify me. They are wide, beautiful, and filled with frightened tears. One of his wings is broken and bleeding, and it hangs limply at his side. Otherwise, the abundance of blood makes it difficult to assess the damage.

Brian collapses into the chair by the doorway and cries silently.

"Beni'," I groan, stumbling toward him, Tim in tow. He moves close to me and pushes Jesse's limp body into my arms. I walk to the back bedroom and lay him on the bed, then come back to Beni', who is leaning heavily on Brian and Tim.

The door slams; Arik comes in, sees the blood, and cries from the next room:

"Tim??? Matty???"

Brian is the one who goes to meet him. He is the only one who *can*. It's still daylight outdoors, and it's not safe for Tim and I in the front room. I can hear Brian speaking to him, but I can't make out the words.

I have Tim fetch me a bowl of warm water and a rag, and I cut off the tattered remains of Beni's shirt with the crystal hilted knife at his belt. As I sponge him down, most of the blood washes away, but there's a wound in his side, and it stretches across his chest. It's about sixteen inches long, and though the puncture wound at his side looks deep, it lessens a bit toward the chest.

He is in great pain, although he's trying not to worry me, and I'm careful to be gentle. I take another towel, a dry one, and press it over the wound, then have Tim hold it in place firmly as I go to Jesse.

Brian is holding his head in his lap and crying silently. I touch Brian's cheek and smile at him sadly.

"It's going to be okay," I reassure him, but he shakes his head.

"No, he's *dead!*" I rest my fingertips over Jesse's carotid very gently.

"He's still alive, Brian...but he's been hurt very badly."

"He seems to be coming out of it," Tim opines, as Jesse opens his eyes, and, seeing Brian, manages a smile. Brian weeps with relief.

I find several shallow puncture wounds across Jesse's chest and stomach that don't look too serious.

The majority of the blood seems to be Benediction's.

I bandage Jesse's wounds, all the while noting that Jesse seems much less hostile towards me, unlike earlier in the day. At this point, though, I am much more concerned about Beni'. He is flat on his back, wings beneath him, eyes closed. His skin is pallid, and he's grimacing. The wound has stopped bleeding, and his wing looks better, I notice, as I ease him into a sitting position. I gently palpate the bases of his wings with my fingertips, around the hollow bones which form the outer frames of them, and lastly, the feathered surfaces which stretch over the flesh inside them.

Beni' clenches his teeth and moans a bit, but is otherwise silent. I take his arm and shoulder on the wounded side, gently testing the range of motion. Beni' grunts, and tears squeeze out of his eyes.

"I'm *sorry,*" I say kindly, "But we're going to have to make a brace of sorts. It will make you more comfortable."

Timothy smiles at me as he brings me the tape and bandages and sits beside me on the bed. I smile back at him and I get to work immobilizing Beni's arm and shoulder in the correct anatomical position. Tim brushes the hair away from my brow and kisses it.

"You're remarkable. Wherever did you learn to *do* that?"

"Matty never told you?" Beni' groans. "He was quite the *physician* in his mortal days."

"That was a long time ago, Beni'," I tell him, rolling my eyes. "I've forgotten quite a bit."

"The man is *brilliant,*" Benediction affirms, and I feel myself blushing once more. Beni' can *always* make me blush. "An excellent surgeon, as well."

"Can I get you anything, Beni'? Water, aspirin...tape for your mouth?"

Beni' chuckles, then groans.

"Shut *up*. It hurts to laugh."

I am suddenly very weary.

"Come on," Tim says, pulling me to my feet. "Let's go to bed."

Beni' catches my hand, and I bend down to him.

"What is it, Man?"

He smiles, and closes his eyes.

"Thanks, Matty..." he groans with discomfort, and then opens his eyes and fixes me with his beautiful gaze. "I appreciate it," he gasps, then falls asleep.

"Sure thing," I say, very softly, as not to wake him.

"We'll stay with them," Arik tells us. "Get your rest."

"Thank you," Tim grins, and yanks my arm to hurry me out of the room after him.

"Alone at last," Tim purrs, pushing me into the bedroom and kicking the door shut behind him. "You don't know how long this day has been." He pecks my lips, and laughs with delight as I pull a huge bouquet of pink roses out of my jacket and present them to him on bended knee.

"Matty, do you just conjure these things up out of the air?" I kiss his hand, then the tip of each finger.

"The truth? Yeah."

"Well, it's *very* sweet," he smiles, as I push up his sleeve and kiss his inner wrist.

[46]

"Mm, you're tasty," I tease, as I work my way up his arm to his inner elbow, and he giggles.

"That tickles."

"Yeah? Well, look what happens when I do *this!*" I blow hard, and a rather unpleasant noise emits. I erupt into laughter, and Tim stares down haughtily at me, eyebrows arched.

"Well, *that* just ruined the mood," he smirks, rolling his eyes.

"*Aw,* c'mon, Cupcake," I plead, clutching his hand as he turns his back and taps his boot. "I'll behave, I promise."

He pouts. "That was *really* gross."

"I'm sorry, Cupcake," I smile, rising from my knee and taking him gently by the shoulders. "It's been such a horrible day. I needed to laugh a little."

He wraps his arms around my waist and lays his cheek against the narrow 'v' of flesh at my open collar.

"I love you," I smile. "I love *holding* you." I love the silky feel of his hair under my fingertips, his scent--musky and warm, the way he presses me so close, we are almost like one.

"I love you, too."

"But I love *you* more," I tell him, and he slugs me in the chest.

"Owwww!"

"Stop *arguing* with me, Fool. I love *you* more." He gives me that toothy grin again.

I moan:

"Way to prove it, Cupcake, by punching me in the heart. Ow!"

He looks pained for a moment, and then sees through my bullshit.

"Suck it up, Big Guy," he teases, and kisses my chest. "All better?"

"Well, I just don't know," I tease. "You hit me pretty hard."

He pouts.

"Poor Baby! Let me try again."

"Ohhhhh, that's *nice,*" I smile, as he licks my chest, then bites gently. "Damn it, Cupcake, you are just *too* good at that..."

"Glad you approve, Darling," he purrs. "I *do* try."

"You're a *glorious* success." I glance down at his trousers, which are straining forward. "Well now," I smile. "That's more like it." I grasp his hips gently, running my thumbs over his hipbones. "*Come* to me," I groan, and bring his hands to the top of my trousers as well.

"*Mmmm,*" Tim smiles against my lips. "That's delish."

I lick his lower lip, and then tug it gently with my teeth. "Come here," I moan, and close my eyes as he slides the trousers down my slim thighs.

"*Divine,*" he moans, and sinks to his knees before me. His little mouth is hot and wet, and I grasp his head in my hands as he licks me up and down, teasing the length of me, then the tip. He releases me, and grins wickedly. "Grab the *wall*, Matty."

"*WHAT?*"

"Don't *argue*," he purrs. "It's *my* turn." He stands, pecks my lips, and opens the drawer of the nightstand. "So, what flavor do you want?"

I laugh.

"Timmy! Cupcake! I've never seen this side of you--"

"Or I, *you*," he laughs back, and slaps my ass. "Very *nice*...very nice indeed."

"Timmy, I've never uh, been the um--*recipient*, before."

He gives me a sexy smile.

"So, you're a *virgin*, then." He gestures to the drawer. "What kind of lube do you want?"

"G-god, I don't *know*," I stammer, blushing furiously. "Just *pick* one."

He smiles cheekily, eyes sparkling with mischief as I'm standing there, half naked and *dying*.

'That little fuck is really *enjoying* this,' I think affectionately, as he chooses a jar with a saucy grin and bats his eyelashes at me.

"So, what did you find?"

He grins wickedly.

"Banana custard!"

"Absolutely *not!*" I shout, and he grins.

"Just kidding. *Penis* colada?--oops." He blushes, and I roar with laughter.

"Was that a Freudian slip, My Love?"

"Shut the fuck up and bend over, Matty," he laughs, and grabs a warm, wet cloth and wipes me down gently with it. Then I feel his mouth on me, his quick little tongue working as he warms the lube between his fingers. Finally, he whispers, "Ready?" I nod, and he gently and gradually inserts two fingers into me, until they're knuckle deep. "I'm not hurting you, am I, My Darling?" Tim asks softly.

"*Mm*...No, it's a little *odd--*"

"The first time always is," he says tenderly. "Do you want me to stop?"

"No, it feels nice..." He gently moves his fingers in and out, first slowly, then quicker. With his other hand, he grasps me firmly.

"You can come in my mouth, Darling. I don't mind. It's all for you tonight." He takes the entire length of me into his mouth, and I throw back my head in ecstasy. Between his mouth and his busy fingers, the orgasm comes thick and strong, heavy. The world wavers out of focus, and my brow and palms are flat against the wall.

Tim releases me, withdraws his fingers, rinses his mouth and spits in a cup, then turns me to him. His eyes are like green flames, his lips are beautiful, mesmerizing. We kiss, and I feel my knees begin to buckle beneath me. He understands with no need for words, and guides me to a chair. I bend over and grasp the back of it; he warms the lube and rubs his entire length with it, then puts a generous amount inside me as well for good measure.

He kisses my shoulder, grasps my hair at the nape of my neck and purrs,

"Ready?"

"All right..."

He walks to the back of me, trailing his black lacquered nails down my back.

Ohhh. I have *chills*.

I feel him grasp my hips, and I raise my head. I'm startled to see that we're reflected in the mirror in front of us, so distorted is my reality; I don't remember turning from the wall.

Timothy looks beautiful; his eyes are feral, his teeth drawn back in a snarl. He enters me; I feel a flash of fire in my loins, I growl.

Tim thrusts into me with a surprising ferocity. I am mesmerized by his reflection in the mirror, enthralled by it. He is enjoying his power over me, and I love him more than ever. I move with him, taking him deep within me, and I feel another climax rolling up and boiling over...

"*Nnnnnngh,*" Tim groans, and falls across my back, his face in my hair. I feel his hand curl around me, and the orgasm becomes more intense. I let out a shuddering sigh as Tim withdraws from me and pulls me onto the bed.

"Mmmm, that was *nice,*" I purr, as I nestle my head on his chest and smile. His grin is huge, and he puts his arms around me.

"Let me tell you something, Matty," he pants, his heartbeat racing, his breath coming fast. "I may say this quite

[48]

often, but this time I really mean it. You're the *best* that I've ever had! *Truly!"*

I kiss his breast.

"I'm *glad*, Cupcake--because you're stuck with me. For eternity."

He sighs, and leans his chin on top of my head.

"I don't know if my heart could take it," he says, rather seriously.

"Your heart, and my *ass,"* I laugh, and he chuckles.

"You're crazy, Matty."

"And you're ferocious! Who taught you how to make goddamned fuck like that?"

"Who do you think?" He smirks. "Obadi--" He laughs. "*Make fuck?"*

"That's what I said! Whassamatter? You *deaf*, Boy?"

"Matty, don't start talking simple again!"

"But Sweet Pea," I drawl, "Honey Lamb, *Sugar Waffle*--"

Tim lifts the covers. "That's *it*. Go!"

"*Cupcake*!" I wail. "Don't do this to me, Honey Chile, I'm all *nekkid* and shit--"

He wrinkles his little nose. "*Nekkid,"* he groans. "That's the worst one yet!"

"Shut yo' *sass* hole, Boy," I tease, and he laughs.

"Well, okay--you can stay."

"*Yeeeeeeeeee-hawwwwwwwwww*!!!"

"Don't push it, Matty," he laughs.

Chapter Fifteen

The evening rolls around at long last, and I take that opportunity to take a walk with Brian. He is completely miserable. The scent of jasmine hangs heavily about him. This troubled silence is rather unusual for us. I do love this beautiful boy, but as a friend, a companion, a protector of sorts.

"I'm sorry that I hit you," I tell him, finally breaking the silence.

"You *should* be, Matt," he replies, but doesn't look at me.

We continue to walk, hand in hand, and arrive at the fountain in the park where we first met. He doesn't seem to notice; he sits on the bench, and puts his head in his hands.

Deja vu.

'If I had only walked on by,' I think silently to myself. *'I would have spared him this agony.'*

Or, if I would have killed him that evening as I had planned?

"Brian, I'm sorry," I try again. "I'm sorry for *all* of this--"

"*Why* don't you love me anymore?" He lifts his dark head and looks at me, and I can barely look back at him. The pain in his face is like a knife in my heart. I am quite unable to reply. "So, how did you and Tim come to fall in love so quickly? Did you forget about me?" His eyes are glimmering with tears. I touch his cheek.

"No, of *course* not," I smile, rather sadly. "But Timothy completes me. He is a vampire, an immortal. One of these days, you will die and leave me--"

"I was willing to die for you the other night...you know, the night when you killed Timothy! I wouldn't let you leave!"

"Oh, for fuck's *sake*, Brian, that's not fair! You *wanted* to die that night! You *knew* what I was, and you brought me home and we made love...but all along, you were planning your death!"

He bows his head.

"I *was...*"

"But...*why???*"

He shudders, and I take his two hands in mine.

"Brian, tell me why you wanted to die that night."

"I *can't,*" he cries. "You won't understand!"

"*Try* me," I plead, kneeling beside him. "I'm your friend, Brian."

He groans.

"You'll *hate* me."

"I *love* you, Brian."

"The others will hate me too--"

"*No*, Dear..."

"Well, here it is: Timothy has always been in love with me. I knew it, and I've always exploited those feelings to get what I wanted from him. Tim knew deep down that I didn't really love him like that, but he always hoped that my feelings toward him would change. He also knew that I could never live alone, so we stayed together as an unofficial 'couple'. I was so awful to him, I didn't appreciate a thing. I brought my lovers home to our bed--" His voice trails off suddenly, as he sees the anger on my face. "Matty, do you want me to stop?"

"No,” I say tensely. "Go on."

"The previous night, the night before we met, Tim and I had a huge row about it...it was violent. I beat the living hell out of him; he wouldn't hit me, he just yelled a lot, and cried--"

"I didn't notice many bruises--"

"They were there, buried in his *heart,*" Brian grimaces. "Anyhow, I wanted to *really* hurt him, so I remembered him warning me about Obadiah--"

I seize him by the lapels of his jacket, and shake him violently. "*OBADIAH*??? Brian, what did you *do???*"

He cowers.

"I went to the church and asked to speak with him...and he agreed to see me right away. He has always had it in for Timothy for some odd reason, and he knew who I was. I lied; I told him that Timothy was...hurting me--"

"You *WHAT???*" I scream in his face, and then throw him backwards against the bench and begin to pace furiously.

Brian continues: "Obadiah was furious. He raved on and on about what a 'monster' that Tim was, calling him all sorts of vile names, and swore that he would avenge me. He told me that he would protect me. I told him where Tim would be that week, where the client's houses were, and he told me to go to his private quarters and wait for him..."

I sense what's coming next, and I steel myself for it. At this point, I am beyond caring about what happened to Brian, but I'm concerned about my Timothy.

"Momentarily, Obadiah came back, and told me that everything would be taken care of the next evening, and that I should stay there with him and wait until it was 'done'. I am not a thinker, Matt. I just thought that they'd *fight* or something. I had no idea what Obadiah was capable of...or that he killed boys like us. He seemed so nice, so protective...I slept with him to show my gratitude, and he was so tender at first...he's such a fantastic looking man--"

I clutch my abdomen, turn away, and vomit. When I'm through being sick, I weep.

Brian moves to comfort me, but I shove him away violently.

"No,” I growl. "Don't *touch* me."

He pouts, and sits back on the bench. "Very well. Let me finish. Obadiah and I made love to seal the pact. I went to sleep in his arms. That next night, I overheard one of his men talking about Tim, and how he was going to enjoy *'...giving that pompous little fag what he has coming...'* Oh, Matty, they were going to *rape* him first, and then crucify him as a public example. By that time, I realized what I'd done, and I climbed out of the window of Obadiah's chambers and went to the police. They wouldn't listen to me, just laughed in my face. There was nothing that I could do at that point...and I couldn't get the other gypsy boys to help, because I couldn't tell them what I'd done--they would have *hanged* me!"

I raise my head slowly to look at him, the loathing for him showing plainly on my face.

"You *deserve* to hang," I growl, and I feel my fangs cutting through.

He looks steadily at me, his face streaked with tears.

"I know...but I want you to know this...I *did* love you, Matthias."

"I loved you too, Brian."

I get to my feet, and sit beside him on the bench.

"So, why Timothy?" he asks, as I loosen the laces at his throat and pull his hair aside. "Why wasn't I *enough?*"

I embrace him, and whisper in his ear,

"We cannot always choose with whom we fall in love. With Timothy it was like I was stricken with lightning. It was instant...I wanted him to live again so badly."

He gasps as my lips brush his throat.

"And now you want me to die," he intones.

"Yes. You are going to die...and rightfully so."

"I *want* to die," he states simply. "But I want you to allow me one last wish."

I sigh, and release him.

"All right."

"Make love to me, one last time," he begs. "I want to *be* with you."

"That can never be," I say, and he clings to me, trembling.

I embrace him once more, pressing him close. I hate him and I love him.

"Matty, *please,"* he cries.

"I cannot."

"Then allow me to pray," he says quietly, and buries his head in my chest.

How can I deny him that very human privilege?

"Father, please forgive me for I have sinned..."

I listen to him drone on and on, and my heart is heavy. I know that he deserves death, that justice demands it.

"...And Father, please watch over my friends...Arik, Matty, Jesse and Beni', I love them so...and especially Timmy, whom I have wronged so grievously. Show him somehow that I loved him. Protect him. Make him happy with Matty...and never let him find out the truth about what I did to him...it would break his heart..."

I begin to weep, and Brian raises his head.

"It's okay, Matty. I'm *ready* now."

"Brian," I whisper. "I cannot."

"You *can*, you *have* to," Brian pleads. "Matty, do it *now*, while I have the courage!"

I tuck my head under his chin and rest my lips against the side of his throat.

"Matty," he says softly, and I pull back to look at him. He's trembling, and the tears of fright glimmer and flash in his eyes. "Matty, w-will it *hurt?"*

[51]

I squeeze my eyes closed tightly, and begin to sob.

"*Yes*, Brian..."

"It's all over for me now," he says very seriously. "I've dug my own grave."

"Brian, Benediction once told me that forgiveness is an immortal quality, that mere mortals are not truly capable of it."

"Benediction speaks in *riddles,*" Brian pouts. "But you have to do what you have to *do.*"

"Brian, does Obadiah know that Tim is alive?"

"No. He hasn't made a peep of it, if he does."

"*Keep* it that way."

"What does it matter *now???*" Brian cries. "Let me *go*, Matty...let me *die!*" He reaches into his jacket and reveals a sheathed dagger. "I'll do it *myself*, if you won't," he threatens, and I take the knife into my hand, if only to disarm him. He takes my face in his hands and kisses my lips softly and tenderly, then kneels on the ground in front of me. He clasps his hands together once more, and his lips move silently.

I will myself to harden my heart, to have the courage and the strength to do what must be done. I think of my Timothy, my beautiful husband, and the ugly fate that Obadiah had planned for him, and the personification of that act of betrayal is kneeling in front of me. My hands tighten on the dagger as I imagine my Timothy being beaten and raped and nailed to a cross in the town square.

"Never," I utter, teeth clenched.

For the safety of our circle, for the atrocious wrongs committed against my Timothy, he must die.

Resolutely, I move behind him, push his hair forward off of his neck, and clutch the hilt in both hands.

He is strangely calm, and the scent of jasmine is curiously absent.

"There is no life without *you*, Matthias," he intones. "What good is the world without *love?*"

I am sobbing now, but I point the blade straight downwards and focus on a point between the spaces of the cervical spine.

It will be a quick death, at least.

I tense, and am about to administer the death blow, when I hear Jesse speaking to one side of me.

"*I* love you, Brian," he says, as he walks into the clearing and drops to his knees beside him.

Brian collapses into his arms, crying hysterically.

I sway, the earth is spinning. Someone catches me by the elbow and steadies me, and I see my Tim's somber little face. He looks at the knife, and then takes it from me without a word. I begin to cry from deep inside, and Timothy pulls me into his arms. We cling to each other in the sacred dark, I shivering against him, and he holding me tightly.

"Cupcake," I cry, "Cupcake, I almost *killed* him..."

"Shhhh," he soothes. "It's all going to be okay..."

"I almost killed Brian!" I scream. "What the fuck is *wrong* with me?"

"Matthias, you were trying to protect me, and I love you for it, My Darling."

"You heard?"

"Every word. I've known for a long time about what Brian did, but I forgave him."

I sob. "How can you *forgive* something like that?"

Tim kisses my cheek and smooths my hair. "What other choice do I have?"

I lean on him heavily. "*You* are the one who is remarkable," I smile at him, as he leads me home.

Chapter Sixteen

Agony is in my every gesture, my every movement, as I sit on the edge of the bed and bow my head. The tears come up once more, and Tim, standing, embraces my head.

"Shhhhh..."

"Oh, Baby," I cry. "Oh, Cupcake, I'm so *sick--*"

"*Quiet*, now," he soothes. "Just rest."

I'm shivering.

Tim releases me, and begins to undress me for bed. He removes my vest, unbuttons my shirt, and then kneels to unbuckle my boots. There is a knock at the bedroom door, and Tim rises to his feet.

"Just stay here. Don't move. I'll get it." He pecks my lips, and opens the door. "Beni', *what* are you doing out of bed?" Tim scolds him. Benediction looks tired, but his eyes twinkle good-naturedly at Tim.

"I'm *fine*, you little fussbudget," he grins. "Taking good care of Matty, I see."

"Hmph." Tim wrinkles his nose, and goes to fetch a fresh pitcher of water. Beni watches him leave, an amused look on his face, and then turns to me.

"So," he grimaces, as he gingerly seats himself on the bed at my side. "How are you *really?*"

"*Beni'!--*"

"*Come*, My Child," he says gently, and pulls me into his arms. "It's a difficult burden, this immortality business, is it *not?* Forgiveness is divine, 'tis true. But you have *forever* to remember--" He gasps, and I loosen my grip around his waist. "Shhhhh, don't cry now," Beni' smiles tenderly. "You were only doing what you thought was right. Your husband was put in grave danger that night. If he hadn't forgotten his jacket and gone home for it that evening--"

"--I never would have *killed* him!" I cry. Benediction leans his cheek on mine, and holds me close. Despite his injuries, the brace and bandages, his embrace is very strong.

"You saved him from a far more painful death, Matthias. You see, Obadiah has never quite forgiven Timothy--"

"Forgiven him for *what?*" I cry. Beni' kisses my cheek.

"For making Obadiah fall in love with him...and for being a link to his 'sinful' past. He perceives him as a threat to his position in the church."

"But Timothy would *never* speak out against Obadiah! He's *terrified* of him!"

"Perhaps. But Obadiah doesn't know that. He also has another reason to hate Timothy. Your Timothy has one of the most beautiful 'souls' of anyone that I've ever met. He's kind, loving, patient, strong when he needs to be, gentle...and far more 'spiritual' than Obadiah can ever hope to be. He's pure at heart, your Tim." As if on cue, Tim walks back into the room, pours me some water, and perches at my other side. He watches me drink, then takes the glass from me and frowns.

"How are you feeling?"

"Much better," I tell him, as he kisses my cheek and turns to Benediction.

"And what of *you?*" he asks, as he wets a cloth and begins to dab Beni's brow with it. "You're *still* burning up, and yet you're up and wandering about like a lost *sheep* or something!" I snort, and try to cover it up with clearing my throat. Benediction's eyes sparkle, and he grins.

"A *lost sheep*??? Now, *that's* a hot one!" Timothy stops what he's doing and puts his hands on his hips.

"Whatever in the world are you two going *on* about???"

"Nothing, Cupcake," I tell him, trying not to smile, and failing miserably. Tim looks to me, and then to Beni, who is also pressing his lips together to keep from smiling, and shakes his head.

"Certifiable, the *pair* of you." Tim starts to dab Beni's face with the cloth again, and there's another knock at the door. "Will you get it, Matty? I'm rather busy at the moment."

"Of course, Pet," I tell him, and open the door to find Arik looking at me rather anxiously.

"Matty, I'm sorry to bother you, but I thought that you'd want to hear it from me...Brian and Jesse...they were, uh..." His cheeks are scarlet. "...um...they're a couple now."

I roll my eyes. "A couple? A couple of *what?"*

Tim grins, despite his best efforts, and laughter escapes him. "Matty, you're *terrible!"*

I smile wickedly, very pleased with myself, and Arik frowns.

"They were doing it on the kitchen table. *Yuck.*" Beni's face lights up, and he starts humming.

"Beni, what in the *world*?" Tim laughs, as Beni pulls him onto his knee and starts singing:

"Too-ra-loo-ra-lye, too-ra-loo-ra-laddie," in a really bad accent, and laughing like an old drunk. "Aye! Yeh never-r-r hear-r-rd that ol' song, Courtin' in the Kitchen? Oh, me ol' Boyo--"

"Beni's *lost* it," I laugh, as Tim tries to get up, and Beni' sweeps him backwards into his arms.

"Oh, but ye be a *fair* laddie!" Beni' yells, and Arik widens his eyes.

"That has to be the *worst* Irish accent that I've ever heard!"

"Poor *Tim,"* I grin, as Beni' covers his face with kisses and then finally lets him up. Tim, of course, is thoroughly disgusted, and tries in vain to scrub Beni's coral tinted lip gloss from his cheeks.

"You ruined my makeup, you *clod!"* he spits, and throws the rag at Beni', who catches his hand, and pulls him onto his lap, gently this time.

"I'm sorry, I was trying to cheer you up," he says, very seriously, as Tim begins to sniffle a bit. "I'd forgotten that after Obadiah, you'd become a bit sensitive about being forced into a situation, and about being physically restrained. Please *forgive* me, My Child. I love you. I wouldn't hurt you for the world..." Tim begins to sob, and Beni holds him gently. "*Shhhh,* don't cry."

There is a timid knock at the door, and Brian enters. He goes to Tim without a word, and hugs him from behind.

"Brian, I'm okay," Tim tells him. "Don't *worry,* all right?"

At the sight of Brian, I begin to feel sick again, and the floor rushes up to meet me very suddenly...

~*~*~*~

...I awaken flat on my back in bed. Arik is sitting at my bedside; Tim is asleep in a chair on the other side of the bed.

"What happened to me, Arik?"

"You just fainted dead away." He places a cigarette between his lips and fumbles in his jacket for a lighter. I begin to cough, and Arik, catching the hint, puts the unlit cigarette back in his coat. "Matty, you sound *awful,*" Arik winces, his expression very worried indeed. I gesture to him, beckon him closer.

"I-I...talked with Brian tonight," I say with an air of urgency, as another coughing spell takes over. "He *told* me."

Tim, by this time, has awakened, and brings me a glass of water. I choke it down and lean back against him, and he wraps his arms around me.

"He *told* me," I gasp, and begin to cough once again.

Arik catches Tim's eye, and a silent understanding passes between them.

"Everything?" Arik asks, and Tim nods gravely. "Oh, my fucking *faith,"* Arik spits, disgusted. "So what happened?" Arik asks, and Tim quickly shakes his head and makes slashing motions in the air with one hand. I begin to weep, and Tim presses my head to his chest.

"Shhhhh, Matty, it's all right..."

"It will *never* be all right again," I choke, and Tim looks up at Arik.

[54]

"Fetch Benediction, he'll know what to do," he orders, and kisses my head. "Quiet, now..."

"Oh, *TIM!*" I wail. "What if you and Jesse hadn't shown up in time?"

"We heard every word. We never would have let it happen. Don't mourn so."

"How did you *know?*"

"Your unguarded thoughts, My Darling."

I close my eyes, and will my body to stop shivering.

Jesse appears in the doorway, and Tim eyes him warily. I look into his face, and Jesse looks back at me, with his beautiful eyes solemnly shining. Oddly enough, there's no trace of malice in them. Tim's body is very tense, however, and I reach back and draw his other arm around me. He kisses my head again, and the corners of Jesse's lips tug into a smile. Arik, whom by this time has returned with Beni', is watching the silent exchange between Tim and Jesse carefully. I can feel Tim's deep sense of foreboding in his unguarded thoughts towards Jesse, and his protectiveness and loyalty towards me. I also feel the depth of his love for me, and his resolve that he will remain at my side for eternity, come what may. I have chosen well, this extraordinary man who is now my husband. His arms tighten around me, and he gives me a reassuring squeeze.

Jesse sits beside me, and I can feel Tim's anger growing at an alarming rate. Jesse takes my hand in his and kisses my palm. "How *are* you, Matt?" he asks, as he reaches towards me to brush the hair off of my brow. His touch is cool against my skin, and I close my eyes and lean back against Tim.

"Sweetheart, I *forgive* you," Jesse says softly. "We do what we think is best at the time--"

"He's *ill,*" Tim says rather shortly. "Can you make it *quick?*"

Jesse's dark eyes flash with anger.

"Shove it up your *ass*, you little faggot," Jesse sighs, rolling his eyes, and Benediction thunders:

"*ENOUGH!!!* Jesse, Arik--*OUT!* I want to talk to Tim and Matt. Where's Brian?"

"I'll get him," Jesse says, and rises to leave the room.

"Hey," Tim says to Jesse.

"Yeah, what is it?"

"Would you heal Benediction? Matt is in no shape to care for him."

Jesse smirks, and his dark eyes flash once more.

"No. *Benediction,*" his voice is heavy with sarcasm "will have to heal himself."

"Then what good are you?" I ask, remembering Brian's exact comment to Beni' a few nights hence.

The statement has its desired effect. Jesse looks wounded. Beni' watches us carefully, his gentle face troubled.

Jesse's hands are bleeding at the palms, the blood is everywhere. He takes my hands in his, grasping them firmly. There is a comforting warmth, a strength, a power which is transmitting between Jesse and myself. I feel the sickness being swept away from my body like ashes from the hearth, and a strength, indeed a renewal of sorts, emerging to take its place. Tim lets me sit up, and I find myself healed completely.

Jesse smiles, and leans in to kiss my mouth. I turn my head, and his lips brush my cheek instead.

"You're *better* now," he states, and gives Tim a smug look. I can feel Tim's hatred of him...and vice versa. Benediction senses the tension as well.

"Tim, could you help me, My Child?"

"Of course, Beni'. What is it?"

"Could you rewrap my wing? It's caught at an odd angle..."

"Matty can do it a whole lot better than I can."

Beni' pats his cheek.

"Just take your time. You can do it."

"*Oui, I suppose,*" Tim tells him, as Brian comes in, Arik behind him. Jesse's face lights up immediately, and he catches Brian's fingers in his. There is a special connection between the two of them, a strong bond which is even apparent to the mortal eye. Arik watches them, a grin on his handsome face, then pulls out a cigarette and lights it. Beni' is watching them too, as Tim unwraps the base of Beni's wing, and wipes it down gently with a hydrogen peroxide/water mix, and dries it thoroughly.

Brian and Jesse only have eyes for each other. Brian sits at Jesse's side, touches his cheek, and they kiss. We all smile. The kiss is clumsy, but endearing. Brian smiles, and kisses him again, more deeply this time. Strangely enough, Beni', Arik and Timothy are looking at me. I can feel Tim probing behind my psychic wall for a moment, reading my unguarded thoughts. I throw open the doors so he can read me completely. Tim studies my mind: my emotions, my memories, the feelings in my heart, and satisfied, catches my eye from across the room and gives me a smile. I smile back at him, and blow him a kiss. He winks at me, and I get out of bed and cross the room to the two of them.

"Undrape that wound, Cupcake," I order Tim, and he begins to remove the bandage around Beni's middle. The wound is still gaping open, but doesn't look infected. Tim helps me irrigate the rip in his side with the peroxide solution, and then brings me a tray of bandages, tape, and assorted gauze. "How are you doing, Beni'?" I ask him. He looks weary from the fever, but he manages a smile.

"Don't look so worried, Matty. It's not as bad as it looks."

"You need sutures, Man. Quite a few of them. It won't come together properly, otherwise."

Beni pales, and closes his eyes wearily. "Do what you *have* to."

"Beni', there's no anesthetic...and what do I suture you with?"

"I can handle it."

"Beni', you have lost your *mind?* Are you insane?"

"Brian," Benediction calls. "Bring me a bottle of whiskey, Beautiful Child. And Tim, fetch a sewing needle and thread."

"Beni, *no!*" Tim cries, but Beni' holds up his hand for silence.

"Now, we'll have none of *that,*" Beni' smiles, as Tim clutches his hand in the two of his and sobs.

"But Beni', the alcohol will thin your blood--"

"*Buh!* Quiet, Matty! Give that to me," Benediction says, taking the open bottle from Brian, and pouring a generous shot into a glass.

"To liquid courage," Arik says solemnly to Brian, who nods. Jesse watches silently, as Tim gets up to find a needle and thread. Brian sits beside Jesse, his face desolate, watching Beni' drink the whiskey.

"Jesse," he says. *"Couldn't you--?"*

"No," Jesse smirks. "Let him *suffer.*"

"YOU MAKE ME *SICK!*" Tim shouts at him.

"Some divine *grace,* Jesse," Arik mutters, as Tim brings me the thread and the needle, both highly unsuitable for the task at hand.

"Cupcake, do we have any nylon thread lying around? This thread will cause an infection when its wet--"

"I'll go buy some," Arik says, and grabs my jacket. "Can I borrow this, Matt?"

"Sure," I say, rather distracted by Tim, who is pouring water over my hands, and who appears to be deep in thought. "Cupcake, what is it? What's on your mind?"

"Arik, *wait,*" Tim says, and brings my jacket to me. "Darling, do you remember the other night, when you gave me the pink roses? I asked you if you conjured them up, and you told me that you did...do you think that you'd be able to do it *again,* with something *other* than flowers?"

"Cupcake, you're *brilliant!*" I laugh, seizing him in my arms and kissing his cheek soundly. I pull on my jacket and close my eyes, and begin to think of what I'll need: absorbable surgical suture, to minimize risk of infection; a semicircular suturing needle, lidocaine hydrochloride, for the pain; a hypodermic needle, to administer said

[56]

anesthetic...

Though my eyes are closed, I can sense the tension in the room. Everyone's eyes are on me. The absorbable surgical suture, and both needles appear instantly. The lidocaine makes me nervous. The exact chemical composition, the strength...I am unsure. However, I am able to get an approximation, and I fervently hope that it's suitable.

"Matty," Brian tells me. "Beni's *out.*"

I glance down at Beni' from the hypo that I'm filling, and then catch Brian's eye.

"Not for long. He's going to feel *this.*" I administer the needle as gently as I can, but Beni' clenches his teeth and grunts. "A few more of these, and you won't feel a *thing*, I promise, " I tell him, as I systematically numb the wound. He groans in response. The approximation suture comes first, to rejoin the deep tissues in the puncture wound. Then I finish with the apposition sutures, to close the gash. The blood comes freely, and Tim collapses against Arik and Brian, heartsick, tears streaming down his face. "It's okay, Cupcake," I smile up at him as I work, the technique coming back to me rapidly. Benediction doesn't appear to be in pain anymore, but he still looks tired. "Beni'," I say, suddenly overcome. "Beni, what can I *do* for you?" Benediction closes his eyes wearily, and puts his hand on my arm, squeezing gently.

"You're *doing* it, Matty..." Tim begins to sob again, and Beni' sighs. "My Darling, My Little One...come to me." Tim goes to him, and cradles his head on his lap.

"Beni', you've been hurt so badly..."

"We *all* have, My Child," he tells Tim, gazing lovingly up at him.

Tim strokes his cheek. "Oh Beni', I *do* love you so..."

"My Lamb," Beni' smiles affectionately. "Always worrying about everyone else but yourself...you're a good man. Did anyone ever tell you that, or were they too worried about themselves? I know that your life has not been a happy one, but you've handled it with such *grace*---"

"*Amen,*" Arik affirms, and Brian nods.

"Yes."

Jesse scowls, but remains silent.

"Tim, help me with this *bandage*, will you?"

Tim sighs, and kisses Beni's forehead.

"*Merci*...thank you," he smiles at Beni', lips closed.

"You're welcome," Beni' groans, as we ease him up very gingerly and I apply the topical antibiotic.

"Almost through now, Man, just hang in there." Beni nods weakly, and leans on Tim as I begin to dress the wound and finally wind the bandage around him.

"You *could* have healed him," Brian frowns at Jesse, who suddenly looks very weary indeed.

"Brian," he sighs. "You'll *never* understand." Brian brushes a strand of his hair back and touches his cheek.

"*Try* me." He guides Jesse's mouth to his, and they kiss once more, softly at first, and then so passionately, that I feel a stir in my belly. I look over at Tim, who is watching them as well. His face is soft and dreamlike, and his hand is resting on his chest lightly. His eyes hold a look of intense longing, and I smile to myself. Tim feels me looking at him, and blushes immediately, lowering his long, natural lashes and smiling at the floor.

Suddenly, I'm feeling very frisky *indeed.*

Arik is grinning from ear to ear.

"Wow! Look at 'em *go!*"

"*Arik!*" Benediction gasps in mock horror, trying not to smile and failing miserably. "*Shame* on you!"

"Sorry, Beni', don't know the *meaning* of the word," Arik says, his voice as dark as velvet as he sits at Beni's side and studies him, blue eyes smoldering. To my surprise, Beni' pulls him close with his good arm and laughs.

"Come here, *you,*" he smiles with affection, and kisses Arik's lips. Arik kisses him back, and then slaps his chest playfully.

"*Naughty* boy!"

I wiggle my eyebrows at Tim, and he grins back at me, looking a bit sheepish. I sweep him off his feet and into my arms instantly.

"Put me *down*, Matty!" he shrieks, as I smooch him loudly for dramatic effect.

"Nothing doing, my sweet little Cupcake!" I yelp triumphantly. "You're mine, *all* mine!"

He rolls his eyes at me.

"Oh, *brother.*"

I glance around the room, but both beds are occupied, and the chairs look extremely uncomfortable for the task at hand. Sighing, I hoist him up again, and head for the door towards the back bedroom.

"Please put me down, Matty!"

"I'd *love* to. You weigh a *ton!*" He slugs me. *"Ow! Cupcake!"* I deposit him on the bed, flat on his back, and gaze down at him. "You are *divine*," I say, quite seriously, as I study his beautiful face, softly framed by his shining chestnut mane on the pillow. "Your beauty is more intoxicating than wine..." I bend over to kiss his lips, and right before our lips meet, he smiles, and murmurs:

"Well, there's enough *cheese* to go with that wine..."

I chuckle. "Mm. Shut up."

He grabs my lapels and pulls me down on top of him. "*Make* me."

"Ohhh, I *plan* to, Cupcake. I *plan* to..."

Suddenly, Jesse walks in, without knocking, and perches on the bed, staring at us.

"*Excuse* me, but this is our bedroom--" Tim begins, but Jesse interrupts him.

"No, it's not. Its Brian's and mine," Jesse smirks.

Tim frowns.

"*As* I was saying, this is *my* home," he says sharply. "We'd appreciate it if you'd *knock* first." Tim's voice is very stern.

"Bite my *dick*, you uptight little uberfairy," Jesse snarls, and then leaps back just in time to avoid my fist connecting with his jaw.

"APOLOGIZE! *RIGHT NOW!!!*" I thunder at him, and he groans as I grab the shirtfront of the dress and shake him. *"SAY IT!!!"*

"*Sorry*," he mumbles, not looking at Tim, who is staring at him with undisguised hatred.

"Apology accepted. Now get *out* of here! This is *my* house, and what I say goes! *Got* it?" Jesse glares at him, and to my surprise, Tim leaps out of bed and jabs his finger at him. "Are we *clear???*"

"*Yes*," Jesse mumbles sulkily, and Tim snarls at him.

"Good! Now leave us." Tim wraps his arms around my waist from behind, and gives me a reassuring squeeze. Jesse throws us one last withering glace over his shoulder, then slams the door with a loud bang.

"I wonder what he wanted," I muse, as Timothy turns me to face him.

"I don't *care,*" he smiles dreamily, as he encircles my neck with his arms. "Now *kiss* me, before I *die* of wanting you!" He raises his little face, closes his eyes and pouts. I lift his chin and peck his lips.

"What about the others?"

"In a *moment,*" he smiles, and brushes my lips with his, gently at first, and then the kiss becomes more ardent. He presses me close, removing my shirt, and digs his long, lacquered nails into the flesh of my back. "Matthias," he moans, as I struggle with the laces at the front of his shirt, and then peel the wide neckline down from his shoulders.

"What *is* it, Cupcake?" I murmur into his ear, as I breathe in his scent, warm and musky. He pulls back and smiles at me, fangs cutting through.

"I'm *famished*, My Pet."

"I'll go bolt the door," I grin, and do just that.

"Mmmmm...Matty," he pouts. "You're making me *wait...*"

Brat.

"One minute, Cupcake," I tell him, and go to my jacket, which is hanging on the modesty screen to the side of the bed. I reach inside, and produce a single, long stemmed rose, as red as heart's blood. He takes it from me, smiling, and kisses it, enjoying its heavy scent. I smile back at him, and he embraces me once more.

"You've *never* forgotten," he smiles tenderly, and pecks my lips.

"A *promise* is a promise," I murmur into his ear, and then I take his left hand in mine and kiss it, studying his wedding band. "And a *vow* is a vow."

His eyes glimmer with tears. "Oh, Matty, I *do* love you so!"

I lift his chin and smile at him tenderly. "I love you too, Cupcake." My fingers fan over his cheek, and I guide his lips to mine. He groans from deep inside of him as I kiss him deeply.

"I'm *hungry*, My Darling," he whispers, face upturned in ecstasy as I kiss his ear, his throat, the nape of his neck. The roar of his blood under his flesh becomes apparent as my fangs cut through. This is an ancient custom among immortals, to feed upon one another in times of short supply, or in cases of moral or temperament issues, or in our case, the joy of communion, of sharing the gift of one another's bodies. The closeness that we feel transcends the sweetness of mere sexual pleasure. It is becoming one with that person, one body, and one mind. It is a marriage of flesh and blood, a rapturous affirmation of eternal life.

I allow him to lead me to the bed, and we sit together, he cradling my cheek in his hand, and looking at me tenderly. "Matty, every day, I am so glad that you've chosen me...My *Savior,*" he says, very solemnly. His eyes are brilliant emerald green, boring holes into my soul. "I do adore you, My Darling..." I gasp as his lips press against my throat, and I feel his lips stretch into a smile. "Mm," he whispers. "All mine...every *drop* of you..." He nips me, and begins to feed, his hot little mouth wet against my flesh, and I shudder with pleasure.

"Tim," I groan. "Oh, My *Darling...*" I rest my cheek against the top of his head, and he presses me closer. I close my eyes when he finally draws back and licks his lips, his hand still on my cheek.

"Matty," he smiles, as he turns and looks back over his bare shoulder at me, and I grasp his upper arms from behind and kiss his ear. He is now the prey, and I the hunter...or is it the other way around? I care not.

"Tim," I groan yet again, as I press my lips to the nape of his neck and rub my face in the silken glory of his hair. My arms encircle him firmly; he grasps my arms and leans back into me.

"My *heart*," he whispers, as he leans back and presses his cheek to mine.

"Mm?" I murmur into his ear, as I bite the lobe, then tug gently. I find the jugular, and nuzzle his throat, then turn him to face me. I kiss him deeply, longingly, never wanting to let him go. He breaks our kiss with a gasp, and smiles, eyes closed.

"My *heart*, Matty," he pants, and I lay him back on the bed.

"What of it?" I smile, as I peck his lips, and thrust my face deep into his throat. He takes my hand and kisses the palm. I feed with ravenous hunger, then pull back to look at him. He smiles up at me, lips closed, and I peck his lips once more.

"Feel my *heart*, Matty," he says, and I lay my palm over his chest. He covers my hand with his, and I kiss his lips gently, then his shoulder, and finally the flesh of his chest, which stirs with each heartbeat. Tenderly, I rest my head there, and close my eyes. He sighs deeply, and smooths my long black hair with the palm of his hand.

"Matty, are you *asleep*?" he asks me, after a while, and I smile to myself.

"Yes."

"Matty!"

"Shhhhh," I smile, and rest my hand on his flat belly. "You wouldn't want to wake me *up*, would you?"

He snorts. *"What?"* he laughs, and I frown.

"Don't *shriek* so," I say drowsily, and smile against his flesh.

"You're *not* asleep, Matty."

"Are you *certain*, Cupcake?" I ask innocently. "I could be talking in my sleep, you know."

He sighs, and encircles my shoulder with his arm.

"Matty, what are you *up* to?" he laughs, as I reach over and begin to toy with his nipple ring, then snuggle my cheek deeper into the flesh of his left breast and smile. "*Nothing*...I'm asleep."

"You are *not.*"

I chuckle.

"Am *so.*"

"Fine," Tim sighs. "Sweet dreams, then."

We lay in silence for twenty minutes, and then Tim kisses my brow.

"Matty?"

"What is it, Cupcake?"

"What is it about me that you love so?" He rubs my back, and I sigh, contented. *"Matty?"*

"I'm *thinking,*" I smile. "*Give* me a minute." He smiles at me as I raise my head to look at him. "You're breathtaking," I reply, smiling back at him.

He caresses my cheek, and then presses my head to his chest with the palm of his hand. "I love your simplicity, Matt, " he tells me. "And you're strong."

I kiss his breast, and then rest my hand upon it once more.

"Your *heart* is strong," I smile, as I gaze into his eyes. He smiles at me, mouth closed, and I peck his lips. "...like a hide drum. I could listen to it all day..." I kiss him again, deeply, and move on top of him. His arms come around my waist, and we hold each other tightly.

"Matty?"

"Mm, what is it *now?*" I moan, my lips pressed to his throat.

"This isn't even our bed."

I ignore him, and begin a trail of kisses, from the hollow at the base of his throat, the center of his chest, his flat belly, his pelvic bones...I unbutton his trousers, and slide them down his thighs, pull off his boots and his high cuts, and kiss the little concave area below his navel. He giggles most appealingly, and I feel myself growing engorged, lost in his soft, white flesh.

"That's *nice*, Matty," he whispers, and I smile, as Tim's body responds to my touch.

"You're tellin' *me*, Darlin'," I reply huskily, and I rub my face in the hollow of his hipbones.

"Oh," Tim gasps, as I take one of his thighs gently from beneath and bite the inside of it, then take the other and do the same.

"You're so *pretty,*" I whisper, my voice smoky with desire. "How beautiful you are, My Darling..." I moan, and take him deeply within my mouth. He arches his back and grabs two handfuls of my long black hair, and we move together like music.

"Oh, Matty," he pants, and erupts, screaming, his limbs trembling with exhaustion. I hold him in my mouth until he's through, then release him and swallow. He is still flat on his back, panting, as I reach into the nightstand cabinet for some whiskey to rinse my mouth with. I offer him some, and he sits up and takes it from me, smiling.

"Come here," I smile, as he perches carefully on my knee, and embraces me around the neck.

"Matty, there isn't *room,*" he grins, blushing furiously. "It's so *big.*"

I glance down at my rather impressive trouser bulge, and give Timothy a playful squeeze around the waist.

"Will you take care of that for me, Cupcake?" He presses his lips together and complies, grasping me in his hand through the slacks. I lean my head against him as the friction becomes more intense; he gives me one final burst of energy, and I come like a freight train, my reality temporarily suspended. When I regain my bearings, he is softly and sweetly in my lap, his legs around my waist, and his arms around my neck. His green eyes are very bright, and he is watching my face intently. "Tim," I purr, my voice still husky. "What have you done to me, My Pet?" He gives me a cute little tight-lipped smile, and rests his brow on mine. I nuzzle him, and kiss his mouth.

"Now, Matty...this isn't even our bed," he repeats, as he lifts his chin so that I can kiss his neck. I take his nipple ring in my mouth and suckle.

"*Awww...whassamatter*, Butter Biscuit?" He slaps my chest playfully.

"Why, nothing! I--*Butter Biscuit*?" He rolls his eyes. "Matty, why do you *do* that?"

"Mm?" I ask, taking his other nipple ring between my teeth and licking him gently. "Oh, you're pretty," I groan, as I lean my head on his chest again. He grasps my chin and lifts my face to his.

"Why do you *do* it?"

I touch his cheek gently with my fingertips. "Do *what*, Cupcake?"

"*This*, Matty--" He makes a bizarre face at me, eyes crossed, teeth jutting forward. "*Hyuk! I wanna make fuck wit' yew the whole night through, mah lil' sack o' sour mash!*" I stare at him, and he drawls: "*Ah wanna spark wit'choo 'til the sun come up, mah lil' possum pie!*" He frowns at me. "Is that *sexy* to you?"

I am dumbfounded. There is a moment of silence as I weigh the question heavily, with the serious consideration that it deserves. I study Tim's face, the pouting lips, the glinting eyes, and I finally make my decision.

"Hell, *YES!!!*" I holler, and push him on his back, laughing hysterically as I leap atop him and bury my face in his throat.

"Matty, you're *crazy!*" Tim shrieks, laughing, as I pin him to the bed, holding his wrists together over his head.

"Shut up and *kiss* me, Butter Biscuit."

He snorts.

"Oh, I'm *swooning.*" He starts to pull that goofy face again, and I frown.

"Didn't your mother ever tell you that your face would stay that way if you made faces like that?"

"*Doy!*"

"Cupcake!" I laugh. "Will you *stop?*"

"It's kind of *fun*, actually...*duuuh!*"

"*Tim.*"

He beams at me, every tooth in his head clearly visible. "*See?*"

I shudder.

"Indeed. That was *horrific.*"

"What time is it?" Tim asks, and I glance at the wall.

"Eight PM."

"I've got to bathe and dress for work," he smiles. "We should rouse the others."

"Go *ahead*, Cupcake, I'll wake them up."

He pecks my lips, and gathers his clothes over one arm, and mine as well. He deposits them in a hamper by the door, and disappears into the bathroom. I exit into the hallway, and run into Brian, who has the sheets from the bed in his arms. He gapes at me for a moment with fright, then swallows hard, and walks by me without a word. He deposits the sheets in the hamper in the room, and crosses his arms over his chest, as if he's felt a sudden chill.

There is a heaviness in my heart as I turn away and walk up the hallway to Tim's and my bedroom. Benediction and Arik are still sleeping, and Jesse is busy putting new sheets on our bed.

"Thanks," I tell him, and he gives me a baleful look. "Listen, there is no need to be this way," I tell him. "What has gotten into you lately?"

[61]

"I'm *tired*, Matthias...and it's really none of your business."

"It is, when you're bothering my husband and my friends...and trying to turn Brian against Benediction. It's just *wrong*, Jesse. Beni' is one of the dearest people--"

"Beni' is a *traitor,*" he snarls. "He was my father's favorite, and he *turned* on him!"

I close my eyes wearily.

"Jesse, he was *trying* to do what was right. Your father felt as if he had to answer to no one. He killed millions of people, put them through all manner of ridiculous tests to prove their loyalty to him...and *you*, Jesse, you *too* tried to reach your father. You begged on behalf of all humanity, and you even offered *yourself* as the ultimate sacrifice..."

"And look at where it *got* me," he says, his eyes shining with unshed tears, as he unbuttons the front of the dress and shrugs it off of his shoulders. Up close, I see the extent of the abuse, the scars.

"Jesse, I *want* to understand," I plead, and I draw him into my arms. His body is rigid and stiff with distrust, but he leans his head on my shoulder. "Jesse, look at what he's *done* to you..." I run my fingertips over the deep scars in his back, and I feel tears stinging my eyes as I envision the physical pain that he must have endured. "Jess, please *talk* to me."

"What do you want to *know?* It was just as Luci--*Beni'*--said. I spoke to my father about giving my blood in return for the sin of mankind. He finally agreed. I walked the earth as a mortal for a short period of time. I brought many souls to him, but made many enemies as well. I was tried and crucified. When I left my mortal life behind me, I returned to heaven, so pleased to see my father once more. He told me that I handled it with grace, and embraced me..." He pulls back to look at me, his dark eyes haunted and filled with grief. "Then he cursed me for 'defying' him, for telling him that he was wrong and unjust...he had the skin scourged off my body, and as I lay at his feet, he cut off my wings with a sword. The *pain,*" he groans. "There is nothing like it. He told me that I was no longer his son, and that I belonged to Lucifer, that I was damned."

"How did Benediction react to you, when you appeared in Hell?"

Jesse sighs.

"He just looked at me at first, kind of shocked. His lips trembled, and he began to sob. *'My Poor Child, oh My Darling,'* he said, and lifted me into his arms. I thought that he was taking me to the fires of torment that my father had spoken of to mankind, and I prepared myself for the worst. He didn't. He enveloped me in his wings, and I was healed. I was very ill for many days, and he cared for my wounds. I stayed with him for years, until I heard that my father was dead in the hearts of the men he created. That's when I started hearing the prayers of mankind, and realized my mistake in trusting Luce. He is the father of lies, the corrupter--"

"He *healed* you," I say incredulously, but Jesse bows his head.

"Yes, but he is *separate* from my father. He is unwholesome."

"Jess, so are *you*, by that deduction."

"I *know*," he tells me softly. "But I am the sole hope of humanity now."

I put my arm around him.

"What a heavy burden to bear *alone.*" He allows himself to lean on me for a moment, and looks down at his clasped hands in his lap.

"You want to know what the *worst* thing is? People don't understand that I'm not my father, that I'm not going to punish them. There is no Heaven, or Hell for that matter, at least for mankind. When they die, it's *over* for them."

"Except in the case of resurrection."

"That requires Old Magic," Jesse informs me. "And it's not always successful."

"I had my doubts about Tim."

Jesse sighs.

"So did *I.* That's why I showed up that night. I heard Brian's prayer."

"Then I suppose that I have *you* to thank for Tim's life."

"I did it for Brian," he says, pulling away very suddenly and getting to his feet. "He needed a chance to apologize to Tim for what happened. He needed to feel that forgiveness from him."

"Brian received that right away," I state rather proudly. "He is a remarkable man, My Tim."

Jesse buttons up the front of the dress and checks his reflection in the mirror before turning back to me.

"Yes, he *is*. A whore with a heart of gold. How *original*, and how twisted..." He smirks. "Just like my father. He loved paradox. After all, am I not the ultimate example? I am a man, but I love to dress like this. I enjoy the companionship of other men, and my father made that a sin. Isn't that ridiculous? He created people with certain characteristics just to *hate* them. The very worst paradox is this: I love mankind...and they *hate* me. I am all about love, but all that they can see is *law...*"

Jesse looks up as Tim walks in, looking like a beautiful, Gothic vision of perfection in black latex, patent, and lace.

"Jesse," Tim says, absently, and turns to me. "Matty, what do you think of these pants?" he asks me, turning to the side so I can see the grommets and laces on the outer thigh running up the entire length of his leg. "Do they *fit?*" I stifle a moan, as my gaze travels to the heel of his platform stiletto boot, and slowly upwards to the laces at his groin. *"Matty!"* Tim frowns, tapping his boot with impatience. *"Whatever* are you staring at?" I grasp his hips and pull him to me.

"If you have to *ask*, Cupcake--"

"No!!!" he shrieks, turning his head as I lean in to kiss him. "It took me *twenty minutes* to apply this makeup!" He holds me away with his black velvet gloved palms flat against my chest. I release him reluctantly, and he straightens out the black lace shirt and the thin leather trench.

"Hey, you look *great,*" Jesse offers, and Tim gives him a blank look, before applying a touch of black liner to his catlike green eyes.

"Love the base shade, Cupcake," I smile.

"Its 'marble'," he tells me, as he retouches his lips with shiny black gloss.

"Tasty," Brian grins at him from the doorway, and Tim smiles.

"*Thank* you."

Tim leaves the room, and two seconds later, a resounding wolf whistle rings through the air, and we hear Beni' scream:

"Owwww! Yes!!!"

"Hell, Ja!" Arik pipes in, and they break into applause. Tim laughs, and comes back to the bedroom, blushing madly.

"Well, I do believe that you are a *glorious* success," I tell him, as Arik and Beni' stumble in after him, tongues on the floor, and stop dead when they see me. The result is comical. They both start clearing their throats and coughing, and Arik hurriedly covers himself with a throw pillow from the chair.

"Oui...apparently so," Tim smiles, taking my arm. "Shall we go?"

"Shouldn't I *change* first? My trousers aren't...clean."

"Oh?" Tim looks up at me, and then covers his mouth with his gloved fingertips and widens his mascaraed eyes. *"Oh! Oui-oui*, by all means," he blushes, and I go shower.

Chapter Seventeen

"So Timmy, what's the occasion?" Arik asks him, as I reenter the room, clad all in white, from platforms to the white lace choker with the silver ankh.

"A special client," Tim smiles, as he hops in the makeup chair and crosses his legs. "*Fabulously* wealthy. Wants several of us."

"I'll go," I say hurriedly, and everyone nods.

"I'm going too," Benediction states.

"So am I," Arik adds, "To look after Beni'."

"Jesse and Brian are coming too," Tim smiles, and Brian smiles back at him.

"Well, if you *insist,*" Jesse says, and Tim gives him a tight-lipped smile.

"I *do*. Well, we have an hour before he expects us, so everyone look *lovely*!"

"Don't *ahhh* always?" I drawl, and Tim slugs me.

"*None* of that!"

"*Ow*," I whisper, and he rubs my chest.

"I'm *sorry*, Matty, but we must mind our manners and be gentlemen--"

"*Fuck Ja,*" Arik snorts, and bows deeply at the waist before Tim. "*I'll* remember my goddamned manners, ya *bastard!*"

Beni' seizes him by the back of the collar and pulls him backwards.

"Now, *behave,*" he scolds gently, eyes twinkling.

"We'll have none of *that,*" Tim scowls, repeating himself, and I cackle.

"Calm *down*, Timmy. We'll make you proud."

He glares at me, and then snickers.

"Matthias, I have every confidence in you--"

"*Awwwww* Baby, thank *yeeew--URK!*" He grabs me by the collar and smiles, showing every tooth to me.

"--because I will make you *sorry*, otherwise."

"Mercy!" I squeak.

"You *tell* him, Honey," Beni' teases, and we all laugh.

~*~*~*~

By the time the horse drawn carriage arrives for us, we've all made ourselves as stately as we're ever likely to get: Tim, as always, regal and well-bred, dressed in black; I in white; Benediction in cream; Arik in blue; Brian in purple; Jesse in fiery red. Heads turn as we travel past, but turn back just as quickly as they catch my eye.

"So, who *is* this guy?" Jesse asks Tim, who shrugs.

"I know not. I didn't speak with him directly, but he seemed very kind on the phone."

"Well, he's *rich*, anyhow," Arik grins, and Tim rolls his eyes, mortified.

"*Please*! Behave yourselves!"

"*Yeth*, Mommy," Jesse squeaks, and we all erupt into laughter as Tim shakes his head, muttering.

After fifteen minutes, we pull up to a large, colonial-style home. It is absolutely lovely, with a large fountain sculpture of two serpentine water dragons on the curved cobblestone entry walk, and a thick brace of trees surrounds acres of emerald green, perfectly manicured lawns and hanging gardens. Marble benches are scattered about, and there is even a pond with beautiful black swans gliding gracefully across the surface of the water. Two men come to meet us; one tends to the horses, the other to us. He is young, no more than sixteen, with a cleanly handsome Asian face.

"You are most welcome here," he smiles at Tim, and bows. Tim puts his fingers over the boy's hand and steps down from the carriage with elegance, his head held high.

"Merci," Tim smiles, and the boy blushes. He offers his hand to Benediction, who, with some difficulty, manages to exit the vehicle with dignity, although he is still in pain from his injuries. Arik and Brian are next, and then Jesse, and I step down last.

"If you will follow me, please," the boy smiles, and he leads us through the double-doored entrance hall and into a sitting room. It is richly Oriental, red and gold, and black lacquer, and the rugs are of such a quality as I have never seen before. I wander about the room, hands clasped behind my back, enchanted by the jade and ivory carvings and the beautiful woodwork, completely unaware that I'm being observed. Tim is frantically trying to get my attention from across the room, and at last succeeds, but he's also drawn the attention of our hosts as well.

"Relax, Little One," the tallest one tells Tim, who smiles, and clears his throat.

"We are honored to be here," Tim says, as he takes the hand which is offered to him. "I'm Timothy, and these are my boys: Arik, Jesse, Brian, Benediction, and Matthias...he's a klutz." He wrinkles his little nose, and I open my mouth to say something cutting, and then think better of it. The man laughs, and kisses Tim's hand.

"Would you like some champagne?"

Tim takes his arm.

"Mais oui, s'il vous plait."

I feel jealousy boiling up in me, and I doubt if I'll ever get used to that aspect of Tim's career, but I quickly forget as I'm approached by a cute little guy with pink hair. He is very fine featured, like a doll, and yet he has an air of a street-smart rebel about him.

"I am Hideo," he tells me, studying me with large dark eyes under his fringe of pink bangs.

"I'm Matthias," I smile at him, and he grins.

"Is he *yours?"* he asks, gesturing to Tim, and I nod miserably. He takes a thin, 120 cigarette from a case, offers me one, and then gives me a little half-smile.

"Got a light?" I pull out my lighter, and he gestures with his head to the man with Tim.

"That's Hana-No-Seishin. He's the pretty one. They always flock together."

"I'll say," I reply, my heart sinking, as I see Brian and Jesse join them. "Who is your other friend?"

"That's Yoshiki. Isn't he *something*?"

"Indeed," I smile, gazing at the tall, willowy, graceful man with admiration. He is a classic Oriental beauty: flowing, blond streaked hair, long face, large eyes, beautiful rosebud mouth, golden skin...Yoshiki notices me looking at him, and raises his glass to me. I respond in kind, and sip the champagne, which is very good indeed. Hideo smiles into his glass knowingly, and takes my arm.

"Come. I'll introduce you."

Yoshiki turns from Brian, and smiles warmly.

"Well, *hello* there," he purrs. I manage a smile, and then notice Arik sitting beside Beni', who is in obvious pain.

"Excuse me for one moment," I frown, and I go to Beni', who is leaning back on the sofa, his hand over his side. He is covered in perspiration from the fever, and the blood is soaking through his shirt. "Oh, Beni', I'm *sorry,"* I cry, and he closes his eyes.

"For *what*, Matthias?"

"For allowing you out of bed..."

He sighs.

"I'm a big boy. I can take care of myself."

"I can *see* that," I reply sarcastically, as I lift the shirt and pull it carefully over his head.

"Oh, my fucking *faith!*" Arik gasps, and I groan, as I remove the bandage and see that the sutures have ruptured.

"God *damn* it," I mutter. "How did you manage that?"

"Quite possibly the motion of the carriage, Matty," Beni' gasps, and I shake my head in frustration.

"What will I do? I can hardly suture you *here.*"

"Of course you may," Yoshiki smiles. "Use my bedroom, its more private."

"Thank you," Beni' smiles up at him, and then leans on his shoulder and rises to his feet. Another man, also tall and thin, supports Beni' on the other side. He is very beautiful indeed, with black curly hair, very pale skin, full lips, and large green eyes. His facial bones are exquisite, as are his beautiful white wings.

"Ville," Yoshiki tells him. "Make sure that our guest is comfortable."

"*Si*, of course," he says, smiling at Beni', as he helps him to the bed and sits beside him. *"Siete molto bello,"* he tells Beni', who replies:

"Per questo lo ringrazio, Il Mio Bambino. Siete pure."

"What are they saying?" Arik asks me, and I reply:

"He told Beni' that he is very beautiful, and Beni' said that he was too."

Arik leaves my side, and walks off with Hideo. I sit at Beni's bedside, and Yoshiki asks me what I need.

"A bowl of water, some antiseptic, tape and bandages...I can provide the rest." He brings them to me, and I pull the rest of what I need from my jacket.

"The lidocaine is the worst, isn't it?" Yoshiki says sympathetically, as I numb the wound and Benediction hisses with pain.

"Beni', I'm so very *sorry,"* I soothe.

"Do you have anything for the fever?" Ville asks me, and I explain that I'll give Beni' some willow bark tea when I'm through.

As I suture him, Ville and Beni' chat in Ville's native Italiano.

"Die che cosa equesto?" Ville asks, wondering about the origin of the wound.

"E una ferita della guerra, Mia Bella," Beni whispers. A wound of war.

Ville smiles down at him, pale eyes glimmering like still green water, full lips curved.

"Posso baciarlo pia meglio?" (Can I kiss it better?)

Beni' grins, eyes closed. *"Siete grassetto, Il Mio Bambino!"* A bold one, indeed!

Ville takes his hand in his and kisses it.

"Permettiami di provare," he purrs, and I shake my head.

"Permit you to try? I don't think so. Beni' needs his rest."

"He nesso n divertimento, e?" (He is no fun, is he?)

"No, he's a friend, looking out for me."

"That's right," I say sternly. "I may not be any fun, but I am his friend."

"Devo vado?" (Must I leave?)

Beni' sighs.

"I'm afraid so."

"Kiss me, and I shall take my leave," Ville pouts, and Beni' chuckles.

"All right, come closer to me."

Ville bends over him, and brushes Beni's lips softly with his own.

"Labbra di un angelo! (Lips of an angel!) *Oh, la givia, me non renda il permesso voi!"* (Oh joy, do not make me leave you!)

Beni' smiles up at him, his beautiful eyes deep and dreaming.

"Buona notte, Bambino Dolce," (Good night, Sweet Child) he sighs, and Ville clutches his chest as he extolls:

"Fino al domani, il mio soldato coraggioso! (Until tomorrow, my brave soldier!) *La mi passione, il mio amore!"* (My Passion! My Love!)

I roll my eyes, and Ville blows Benediction a kiss.

"Beni'," I tell him, "You'll have to be more careful this time to stay in bed and take care of yourself--" But Beni' isn't even listening to me. His eyes linger on the doorway where Ville has just exited the room. Yoshiki's eyes glimmer with mischief, and he seats himself at my side.

"I think we have a love match with our Ville and your Benediction."

"Well, it may very well *be*," I say, trying not to smile as I finish bandaging Beni's wounds.

"Perhaps with you and me as well?"

I glance up at him quickly, and Benediction squeezes my hand.

"Go on, Matt. I'll be fine."

"Beni', *no,"* I cry, but Ville has once again appeared at the door.

"Go *on*," Beni' urges me, grinning.

"All right, Beni'...but the two of you need to promise to behave yourselves."

"Bye," Beni' laughs, then groans. *"Ouch!* I can't wait until this damned thing heals."

"It never *will*, if you don't rest," I tell him sternly, but Ville and Beni are already lost in each other's eyes, the outside world so much nonsense now. I laugh, and Yoshiki studies me carefully, smiling.

"You are an immortal, yes?"

"I *am,"* I reply, rather cautiously.

"As am I, and Hideo as well. Hana-No-Seishin is a Nature Spirit. His wings are most lovely."

"I haven't noticed."

"Come with me," he smiles, offering his arm. I take it rather hesitantly, and then walk with him to the next bedroom, where I find my Timothy flat on his back on the silken sheets, Hana-No-Seishin atop him. Hana's wings are very beautiful indeed, much like the wings of a butterfly. They are a pale blue in color, shot through with soft pink, dark blue, and black tones. Hana's mouth is at Tim's throat, and Tim's beautiful face is raised in ecstasy. His eyes are closed, he is panting.

Jealousy rages through me like fire, and when Hana's hand grasps Tim's thigh, I clench my teeth and snarl. Yoshiki pulls me back against him and begins to nuzzle my ear.

"Let's go. We have a quiet room in the back where we will not be disturbed." Gently, Yoshiki turns me back towards the door and leads me into the hall.

"Poor Darling," he soothes me. "Is this your first time?"

"What? No," I reply. "I'm not really a prostitute..."

"All men are," Yoshiki smiles, and the light from the chandelier falls fully on his face, highlighting his gingery blond hair, his golden tan skin, and his startling grey eyes. I cannot help but stare, and he smiles back at me. "What is it, Matthias? Why do you look at me so?"

[67]

"How *beautiful* you are," I sigh. "Such eyes..."

"They are the same color as yours." he smiles, and kisses my hand, his eyes never leaving my face.

"They are *incredible,*" I breathe, and I pull him close to me. "Where are you from?" I whisper in his ear, as I press my lips to his throat and trail my tongue over the hollows of his neck and collarbone.

"Japan, originally..."

"I *love* your accent, your voice..."

He chuckles.

"I love *yours...*"

"What a *beauty* you are," I groan, and toy with the laces at the front of his cream colored, blousy shirt. "Mmmm," I smile, as I draw the edges of it apart, and his eyes twinkle with mischief.

"Would you like this off?" He smiles, and pulls off the shirt and the velvet gloves.

"You have beautiful hands," I tell him, as he unfastens the hook and eye closures under the ruffled lace at the front of my shirt.

"You should see what I can *do* with them," he teases me, and all of a sudden, his lips are on mine, and his body is pressed sweetly against me. I embrace him. He is very slim, but very muscular in the upper body, and his arms are strong. His lips are like fire, and I feel my own blood racing as my body melts into his.

"Incredible," I purr, as he pulls back and leads me to a beautiful bedroom which is strewn with pink, gold and black silk, and leads me by the hand into the ornate bathroom. The shower is beautiful, black marble and glass, as is the large spa tub. The fixtures sparkle with 18K gold, and the ceiling opens to a large skylight above. Here and there, fat pink and black paper lanterns hang lazily, and the wallpaper is shimmering silk in a bold shade of pink. "This is really something," I tell him, and he gives me a secretive smile.

"I have it on good authority that you're fond of cinnamon," Yoshiki says, as he lights a scented oil lamp and begins to run a bath with bubbles. The scent of cinnamon begins to pulsate throughout the room, and I feel heavy, languid. Yoshiki kisses me again, and I kneel before him and rub my face in his belly. His hands cup my face gently as I look up at him, and I slide his trousers down his long, slim thighs, and then remove his boots. He is completely naked, golden as the sun. Beautiful as a sunrise in Elysium. I stand before him; he kneels before me, and peels the white spandex from my thighs. He removes my white patent platforms, and my codpiece, and groans. "Oh, you are all ready for me." I nod. He rests his face against my thigh. His breath is warm upon me, and I am quickly becoming engorged. He stands, and draws my hand to him, and I take it firmly. He gasps, smiles, and leans his brow on mine, and grasps my shoulders.

"Yes," he whispers, as I begin to increase the friction. "Oh..."

"Kiss me," I groan, and he does just that, softly and tenderly.

"Very nice," he murmurs, and we go to the tub and slip under the surface of the water. It's nice and warm, and the cinnamon-scented bubbles are amazing. I allow him to wash my hair, and we bathe each other slowly and torturously, before we make love, among the softly scented bubbles in the fragrant water.

~*~*~*~

Afterwards, we shower, and I pull on a silver silk robe and go to check on Benediction. He is asleep, propped up against the headboard amongst a plethora of pillows. Ville is asleep in his arms, his head on Beni's chest. They make a beautiful picture, the two of them, so obviously in love. I reach over and brush Beni's hair back from his brow, and touch his cheek. He smiles up at me, and I sit down on the bed.

"How are you feeling, Ben'?" I ask quietly, as not to wake Ville.

"I'm good, Matthias, really good."

I touch his cheek, his brow.

"Your fever hasn't gone down."

[68]

"My Dear Child," he smiles tenderly. "My Darling, Don't fret so."

"Shut up," I grin, and he chuckles.

"Dear Matty...I never *could* tell you what to do." He smiles, but he looks tired, older than usual. I take his hand in the two of mine, tears suddenly springing to my eyes. "Matty, what's wrong, My Child? What is it?" I close my eyes quickly, and turn away as the tears come, hot and silent, burning my face and my throat. He squeezes my hand, and I swallow hard.

"Beni', I'm so *afraid...*"

"Afraid of *what?*"

I clear my throat, but my voice is still husky with tears.

"Beni', what if you *die?*"

"I'm not going to die, Matt. You and Timothy will live forever, and therefore, so will I."

I lean against his shoulder, and he rests his cheek on mine, and we sleep.

Chapter Eighteen

A few hours later, I awaken. Its 3:30am. I run a hand through my long, black hair and sigh. Benediction and Ville are still sleeping. Beni looks awful, his face is pallid, and his cheeks are flushed with the fever. I reach over and take Beni's wrist gently in my fingers, and study my watch. Tim comes in, tucks a stray strand of hair behind my ear, and kisses my cheek.

"Good morning," he smiles. "I've missed you." When I don't reply, he sits beside me on the arm of the chair, and crosses his legs. "So, how is he? Is he going to be all right?" There's a lump in my throat, and my eyes sting with tears.

"Oh, Baby, I just don't *know,*" I whisper, and Tim strokes the back of my hair gently with the palm of his hand.

"If *anyone* can heal him, you can, Matt," he says very seriously. "As I said last night, I have every confidence in you."

"Oh, Cupcake," I sigh, as I put my arms around his waist and lean my head on him. "You make me feel as if I could conquer the world."

He lifts my face to his and smiles.

"Dear Matty, I do believe you *could.*" We look at one another, holding a deep conversation with our eyes, and then Tim brushes my lips with his.

"Buongiorno," Ville smiles at us, and Tim blushes.

"Good morning."

"How did you sleep, Ville?" I ask him, and he cuddles Beni' and smiles.

"Molto Bene."

"Good. Be gentle with him. That wound needs to heal properly."

"Si. Delicato."

I smile at Tim, who stands, and brings me my trousers.

"We should think about getting home," I say, "But I don't know if Beni' should be moved."

"We have no *choice,*" Tim frowns, and lays his hand on Beni's brow. Benediction's lids flutter, and he opens his eyes. "You're burning up," Tim tells him, and turns to me. "What's his temperature, Matt?"

"I haven't taken it, Tim, I don't know." Tim rolls his eyes, and goes off in search of a thermometer, and I ruffle Beni's hair. "How are you feeling?"

"Not well, My Child. I'm very tired."

"No better?" Ville frowns.

"I'm afraid not, Bambino Dolce," he smiles at Ville. "Don't worry, I'll be up and about before you know it."

"There is no problem with 'up', *il mio amore*," Ville teases, and Beni' chuckles.

"You are incorrigible..."

"Pervertito," he purrs, and we all laugh as Tim comes back in.

"What's so funny?" he asks, as he shakes down the thermometer, and then holds it up to the light.

"Nothing, Cupcake. Don't look so sour."

He places it under Beni's tongue, and kisses his brow. Beni puts his arm around him and closes his eyes. Tim's eyes are glimmering.

"Matty," he says, voice trembling. "What are we going to *do*?" Beni's arms tighten around Tim and Ville reassuredly, and Tim kisses Beni's cheek. "I love you *so*," he smiles through his tears, and breaks down completely. Ville reaches across Benediction, and takes Tim's hand in his own.

"Don't cry, *Mia Bella.*"

I take Tim's other hand in mine and kiss it gently, trying not to betray my own fears as well.

"It's okay, Timmy," I reassure him, and he shakes his head.

"No don't you *see*? Matty, you of all people should know that he's *dying!*"

Ville leaves Beni's side, and comes over to take Tim in his arms.

"No, no, no, Dolcezza, il mio innamorato, tesoro," Ville soothes, and enfolds Tim in his wings. I swallow hard to disengage the lump rising yet again in my throat, and busy myself with taking Beni's pulse again. Arik comes in, and immediately goes to Tim, who reaches for him and begins to sob once more.

"Matt, what in the *world?"* Arik asks, and I glance up at him.

"Benediction isn't feeling well, Arik."

"Ja, I can bleedin' *see* that," he replies sarcastically. "But *why?"*

"The fever isn't letting go, and it's draining him."

"Is he in danger?" Arik asks me, and I avert my eyes. "Matt, tell me, no bullshit. Is he in *danger?"*

Beni' puts his other hand atop mine, and he nods. I close my eyes.

"Yes, Arik," I tell him wearily, and my Tim begins to wail. Ville's wings droop, and he sits down on the bed, tears flowing silently.

"What's going *on* in here?" Brian asks from the doorway, and comes in, holding Jesse by the hand.

Jesse, his face scrubbed clean of makeup and looking much less fierce than usual, walks toward the bed and stops about three feet away, staring at Beni'.

"Get *away* from him!" Tim cries, trying to pull away from Arik, but he holds him fast.

Jesse's face holds a terrifying jumble of emotions: hatred, pity, and loathing, fear...and finally, resolve. He takes a deep breath, and walks to Benediction's side. He seats himself on the bed, brushes Beni's hair out of his eyes, reads the thermometer, and shakes his head sadly.

Benediction looks at him steadily, sensing his inner turmoil, and then looks at all of us in turn, gathered together in our love for him, smiles sadly, and says:

"My Children, remember that I have *loved* you."

"Beni', *no!"* Tim cries, and breaks away from Arik to embrace Beni's head and cry hysterically. "You *can't* take him from us," Tim pleads with Jesse, who, trancelike, has pulled Beni's crystal hilted dagger from its sheath and is

[70]

holding it in his lap.

"*Peace*, My Child," Benediction says tenderly. "My Lamb. My *Timothy*, so loving, so faithful. You've made me so proud..." He pats his cheek, and Arik comes forward to draw Tim back from him. "Arik, My Protector, so strong. Watch over My Lamb..."

"I *will*, Beni'," Arik says with a strength that he doesn't feel, and turns his head.

"Brian," Benediction calls to the tall, dark haired boy, who is standing alone in the doorway, his head lowered, arms folded across his chest. "Come to me, Beautiful Child." He walks to the bed and sits down beside Beni', but he won't look at him. "Brian, My Love. Don't feel that way. It isn't your fault that I'm to die."

"But how did you know what I was thinking?"

"Your unguarded *thoughts*, My Child." Brian begins to sob, and Benediction embraces him. "Ohhh, My Baby," Beni' soothes. "This is fate; you had nothing to do with it. Don't torture yourself so. You'll have to be strong now."

"I *can't--*"

"Yes, you can. Matty and Tim need you."

"We *all* do," Arik affirms, and Brian breaks down again.

"See? It's not as dark as it feels, Little One." Beni' smooths Brian's long black hair and embraces him, then beckons to me. "Darling Matt, take them out of here, I don't want them to see this."

"What about *me*, Benediction? What about *us?*"

"Matty, I have *always* loved you. From the moment that you were born, and from the moment of your rebirth, your resurrection. We have always been close. You've been one of my great joys, my *dearest* friend...and I need to ask you a favor." He grasps my hands in his. "I want you here with me. Take the others away from this place, and then come back and sit with me." His eyes are beautiful, large and bright, and pleading with mine. "All right?"

"I'm not going *anywhere,*" Tim frowns, with surprising strength in his voice.

"Neither am *I,*" Arik glowers.

"Nor *I,*" Brian states, and everyone looks at Jesse with dread.

"Do not *hate* him," Benediction says gently. "He is his father's son. He knows not what he does. My Children, there is a right time for everything: a time to be born, a time to die; a time to plant, and a time to harvest; a time to kill, and a time to heal; a time to destroy, and a time to rebuild; a time to cry, and a time to laugh; a time to grieve, and a time to dance; a time for loving and a time for hating; a time for war...and lastly, a time for peace. Do you understand me, My Darlings? *Come* to me, for I have *loved* you!" We all do as he commands, this precious *Being*, this loving father that none of us has ever had; this beautiful man with whom we've all shared our souls, our minds, our hearts; who has soothed us, and healed us, and comforts us even now, in the shadow of his impending death. And what an unnecessary death that it is! What *sadness* this room contains, what *grief!* I feel my heart rip in two, and the sobs choke off my breath. I do not have any courage left to fortify Benediction, and I am ashamed.

The scent of jasmine hangs heavily in the air among Brian and Arik, and Ville's eyes plead with Jesse's silently. The tears of an angel are very beautiful indeed.

Jesse's face holds a great sadness, a weariness, and a surprising beauty. His dark eyes are moist, deep and dreaming, and he closes them, his heavy black lashes fluttering as he tries to contain the powerful emotions which beat inside of him.

Benediction studies Jesse carefully, patiently, tears streaming from his eyes as he leans back against me. His skin burns with the fever. He presses his cheek on mine.

"Hold me, Matt, hold me tight--" I encircle him from behind, around the waist. "It *hurts*, Matty..."

I sigh deeply, and kiss his cheek.

"What is hurting you, My Beni'?"

"My heart...his hatred of me...it's an *agony*, like *burning...*"

"Beniamino," Ville sobs, and he crosses his arms across his chest and curls up on his side, his head in Beni's lap. Beni' strokes his back and wings gently.

[71]

"My Darling, *Beniamino*, My Loved One...you have made my final moments so very happy..." He entwines his fingers in Ville's long, shining black curls, and Ville looks up at him with his beautiful face. "Kiss me now, Darling. I need to feel your lips on mine *one* last time, so I can die a happy man--"

Ville sits up, takes Benediction's face in his hands, and kisses him softly upon the mouth. He is crying, his beautiful lips trembling. Beni' brushes his tears away with the back of his hand, and then kisses him deeply. It is a most passionate kiss indeed, and Brian takes the opportunity to move over next to Jesse and whisper in his ear. I cannot hear what they are saying, but Brian is speaking rather frantically to him. Arik is still holding my Tim in his arms, and Tim is weeping quietly, his head snuggled in Arik's manly chest.

Brian is pleading and begging with Jesse, who is sitting rigidly, looking at the knife in his lap. Brian reaches for it; Jesse catches Brian's fingers in his and holds them, and shakes his head. Brian kneels before him, beseechingly, then lays his head in Jesse's lap and weeps.

Jesse's eyes soften, glimmer with tears, as he speaks to Brian, and he puts the knife back in the sheath and sets it aside. Brian weeps still, and Jesse strokes his hair very gently with the palm of his hand.

"It's going to be all right," Jesse tells him, and then catches Benediction's gaze.

Beni's eyes are beautiful, full of love and forgiveness, but they also hold a trace of sadness.

"My Darling," he whispers, and holds out his hands to Jesse, who gently moves Brian to one side, and goes to him, taking Benediction's hands in his own. They sit and look at one another, and then finally, Jesse speaks:

"I'm so sorry, Lucifer...I *misjudged* you--"

Beni' smiles sadly, and closes his eyes.

"You are a boy no longer. You are now a *man.* You are the man that your father never was. You are not his son any longer, you are *mine*..." He groans, as the fever in his body continues to climb. "Would you like that?"

Jesse begins to tremble, and the tears from long ago finally rise to the surface and overflow.

"I'd like that very much, Lucifer--I mean, Benediction..."

"*Come* to me," Beni' smiles, and Jesse crawls into bed beside him and ducks under his arm. "My Son, how I've missed you all these years..."

Benediction is crying, but the age lines around his eyes and mouth are smoothing away, and he's beginning to look like our Beni' again. Brian moves over beside me, and I encircle him with my arm.

"That was a good thing that you did, Bri'. What did you say to him?"

He hugs my waist with one arm, and leans his head on me.

"I simply told him that he was not his father; I told him that he was about forgiveness and love, not fire and eternal punishment."

"You saved Beni's life, Brian. I am forever in your debt."

"Matty, you mustn't think that way. I *love* Beni. I did it for him."

Suddenly, I am overwhelmed with emotion, and I embrace him and cry like a child in his arms. It scares him; the jasmine aura hangs around him briefly, and then disappears. He embraces me in turn, carefully, and leans into me.

All of a sudden, I feel a sharp pain in my heart, a deep sadness. I can feel Tim behind my psychic wall, searching my thoughts, my emotions, and my feelings for Brian. I release Brian and go to my beautiful Timothy, who is trembling with the emotion of the past evening, and I gather his slim frame into my arms.

"Hey there, Darlin'," I say softly to him, my lips in his silken hair. "It's all going to be all right." His arms come around my waist, and he presses his face to my chest and sniffles a little. I catch Arik's eye, and he looks away quickly. His love for Tim is apparent in his smoldering blue eyes. He looks uncomfortable.

I turn my attention back to Tim, and he raises his head to look at me. He looks so weary, my heart moves toward him.

"Oh, Cupcake," I whisper, "Don't *cry...*"

"Matty," he gasps, "Just hold me for a while..." He begins to cry in earnest, and my heart wrenches in two. "Matty, about Beni'...he's still very ill. Are we going to move him?"

"Cupcake, look out!" I cry, as he just narrowly misses the light of dawn streaming through the open window. "Ville, close the curtains!"

Ville rises quickly to do just that, as Hana-No-Seishin appears at the door with Yoshiki and Hide.

"My apologies," Hana says, "It appears that we neglected to wake you in time. Of course, we will compensate you for an extra day, as you are unable to leave with the sunrise. You are most welcome here, of course." Hana's eyes meet Tim's, and Timothy colors prettily and studies the floor, smiling.

Ugh. I feel sick inside. I have missed Tim this past evening, and was looking forward to spending the day with my husband.

'You don't have to flirt with him, you know,' I say silently, inside Tim's head. *'You've done your job already.'*

Tim glances up at me, a pained look on his face, and moves to my side. Yoshiki and Hide exchange worried looks, and Hana crosses the room to take Tim's slender hand in his own.

"*You* are enchanting," Hana purrs, and offers his arm.

Tim gives me an uneasy glance, takes Hana's arm, and mouths, *'I'm sorry, Matty,'* at me.

"You *should* be," I say under my breath, and turn my back.

~*~*~*~

Yoshiki comes into the bedroom which Hana has graciously assigned me, and sits on the edge of the bed. He watches me pace the floor for a bit, then rises to his feet and comes to me, all beauty in his silken pajama bottoms. He is shirtless, his hair casually tousled, his lips a deep blood red.

Oddly, I am not interested.

"Do you wish to be alone?" he asks me, and I nod my head.

"You *are* beautiful," I tell Yoshiki, who smiles at me, and leaves the room.

I study my reflection in the glass and sigh. I am a mess. I pour some water from a large pitcher into a bowl, then slip off the robe and the pants and wash my body. I clean my teeth, then sit before the mirror and comb my long black hair until it shines like glass. I avoid looking into the reflection of my face in the mirror. I want to break the glass into a million pieces, to shatter it, just like my heart. I hurt so badly. My eyes are stinging, and there's a lump in my throat. I bow my head and weep. I lay my cheek on my folded arms on the vanity, and try to catch my breath.

There's a knock at the door, and I raise my head quickly, wiping my face. It is Arik, and he looks rather embarrassed.

"Matt, do you mind if I stay with you today? I just need some sleep--" He yawns hugely, and stretches. "Sorry, I'm exhausted. Hana is insatiable!"

"Of course you may," I tell him, trying not to pout, as yet again, I'm reminded of what my Tim is doing. "It's all good, Arik."

He smiles gratefully, and begins to wash his face and his trunk and arms. I watch him for a while, then get up and go to him.

"Here," I say softly, taking the damp rag from him. "Let me do your back." He pulls his hair forward and turns his back to me.

"Thanks, Matt."

"You're welcome," I smile, as I begin to wash his back with gentle strokes. "Is Tim still with Hana?"

"He is," Arik says softly. "But it's just work, Matt. He doesn't love him like he loves you...he told me."

"And when did he tell you this?"

"A few minutes ago, in the hall." Arik turns to me and frowns. "Matty, are you okay?"

[73]

"I need some whiskey," I say absently, turning from him. "Would you like some?"

"Nah...well, maybe just a little," he grins, taking the glass from me. I pour a generous shot for myself, and sit down on the edge of the bed and watch Arik finish his sponge bath. Arik shakes his head and smiles at me.

"Oh, Matty, you'll *never* change," he jokes, as he finishes his whiskey and takes a seat on the bed beside me. "Matt, don't feel that way," Arik says softly, as I stare down into my drink, miserable. He puts his arm around me, and I lean against him. We sit together for quite a long time, he speaking soft words of reassurance, I crying silently. He pulls me close, and leans into me as well. "Matt, let's get some sleep. You'll be better come nightfall." He eases me down on my back and pulls the coverlet over me. He gazes down on me affectionately, as he touches my face for a moment, then the corners of his mouth stretch into a smile.

"You've changed so *much*, Matt," he tells me, as he climbs into bed beside me. "You never used to *feel*, like you do now...I mean; I was scared for Tim, when the two of you first became intimate. I knew what you were, and what Tim now is. Matty, I *hated* you for taking him from me. Timothy is so special; he's such a warm and loving individual. I was afraid that he would become cold and calculating, as you *used* to be. Matty, I wouldn't have been able to *stand* it, to watch Tim fade away like that...but he has become even more amazing, more loving, more forgiving. He has blossomed like a beautiful flower...Matty?" Tim asks in alarm, as I begin to sob. "Matty, what's *wrong?*"

I allow him to draw my head to his chest, and he holds me tightly.

"I *forgot*," I sob, as Arik rubs my back and tries to soothe me.

"*Shhhhh*, don't cry. What did you forget?"

I close my eyes and try to stop the tears, but they burn in my throat and my eyes and my heart.

"I promised Timothy on the night that he became a vampire, that I would bring him flowers every day...he was so sad that he would never see the sun again..." My voice breaks. "...and I've *broken* my promise..."

Arik sighs.

"The day is young, Matt...the day is young...and so are *we*," he smiles, and brushes the tears from my cheeks with the tips of his fingers. "Come," he says, his voice softer now. "I need someone to *hold* me, to *love* me for once. I need a friend, and so do you. *Be* with me now...no promises, no ties. Just *love* me..." His eyes are bright and beautifully crystalline blue. "...for *now?*"

I smile down at Arik, and brush back his snowy white bangs.

"I cannot make love to you, but it doesn't mean that I don't love you, Arik. I *do*, and I always will."

He smiles. "I *know* that you do, Matty."

I look down at him affectionately, and peck his lips. He kisses me back, and fans his fingertips over my cheek. The kiss becomes deeper, more ardent.

Suddenly, I am aware yet again of a dull ache in my heart, which is growing sharper and more intense by the second. I try to ignore it and concentrate on the feel of Arik's lips on mine, but it feels like a knife in my chest, cutting off my breath. I lift my face from Arik's and sit up on the bed, my hand over my heart. It is rather dark in the room, but I can see Timothy sitting in the chair by the doorway. The light from the chandelier in the hall is flowing over one side of his long, chestnut mane, and the other half of his face is hidden in the shadows.

"Cupcake!" I exclaim, smiling with joy, and I rush to embrace him, but Tim holds up his hand.

"Matty...I'm *hurt*," he says quietly.

"What do you mean, *hurt?*" Arik asks, crossing the room to where Tim is sitting in the chair, and I'm kneeling beside it on the floor. Arik lights the lamp, and the two of us gasp. Tim's face is bruised and bloody, and there are welts and bruises all over his upper body as well. I began to wail loudly, and I embrace him, sobbing into his hair.

"Fucking hell, who *did* this to you?" Arik asks Tim, taking his hands in his own.

"I don't *know*," Tim replies. "I couldn't see his face; it was covered in heavy makeup like a mask. He was tall...and blond...the room was very dark, I could barely see. Hanna had asked me if I could take this client of his, show him a good time, you know? Since he'd paid me for the day, how could I refuse?"

"It's *your* body," I tell him gently, but Tim shakes his head.

[74]

"No, Matty, it's *not.* You don't understand." He cups my cheek in his hand. "This is what I *do.* Anyhow, Hana told me to go wait in the room for him, but not to turn on any lights. He explained that it was what the client preferred. I agreed. I saw the makeup when he stood in the doorway. It was a death mask." He shudders. "He had a strange aura about him. His flesh was cold to the touch, and he was very tense. He never said one word to me; he fell upon me heavily, cut my lip when he kissed me, and then made love to me...and it *hurt!* I made the mistake of crying out, of gasping in pain, and he began to *hit* me...Oh, My *Dear,"* Tim says gently, noticing my distress "It *happens* sometimes. Don't weep, Matty." Arik is crying too.

There is a knock at the door, and I turn my head to find Hana standing there.

"Matthias," he beckons, and I follow him into the hall.

"What *is* it?" I ask rather shortly.

"I have a business acquaintance, and he would like a companion for a few hours. Will you join him?"

I am having trouble keeping the bile from rising in my throat, but I reply:

"What does he look like?"

"He's quite beautiful. Hair like the sun, tall, strong, well made..."

"All right," I tell Hana, and I smile grimly.

Chapter Nineteen

I go to the assigned bedroom, sit at the vanity, and begin to apply my makeup. I fill in my brows, line my eyes heavily in black, and find a pale pink lipstick in an icy pink hue. I generally prefer a deeper color on the lip, but this will have to do. A touch of black shadow on my lids, a bit of mascara, and--*voila!*--I am ready for amour.

As I am brushing my hair, he appears in the doorway. I rise to greet him, my limbs singing with adrenaline.

"Well, aren't *you* a pretty one," he drawls at me, and reaches behind me to douse the lamp. For a second, his face is lit by the lamp's glow, and just as quickly again is obscured by the darkness. He has removed his death mask makeup, and is now favoring a more gothic look. His eyes are thickly lined in black; his lips a deep purple like the bruised petals of a dying flower. Facially, he is one of the most beautiful men that I've ever seen...but his eyes are dark, cold, angry, and as deep and black as wells.

Suddenly, I know who this is, and my heart begins to race with anger. Luckily, the lighting in the room is quite dim, or I'd be frightened that he could see it, trying to burst out of my chest.

"Is somethin' *wrong?"* Obadiah asks me, as he removes his black leather trench coat, and reveals a black silk shirt, which laces at the neck. He's clad from the waist down in black leather, from the pants to the stiletto heeled boots, and the white gold cross pendant dangling from a chain at his belt matches the one at his throat.

"No," I reply, recovering quickly enough to probe behind his psychic wall. When I am satisfied that he has no knowledge of the others, and that he has not recognized Tim from the day's earlier events, I withdraw the link, and try to act sexy, like Tim. I try batting my eyes at him, smiling at the floor and looking up at him, tossing my hair...

Shit.

I realize that I'm *not* a born prostitute. Yoshiki was wrong after all.

"Are you all right, Boy?" Obadiah asks, frowning, as I toss my hair and smile at him. You look like you're fixin' to have a *stroke!"*

'Fuck you, Bitch,' I think silently, but smile innocently instead. "It's my first time," I lie, knowing how he dearly loves the feeling of domination over someone weaker.

His lips stretch into a satisfied smile, and I resist the urge to slap his face.

"Oh, *really*, now..." He grasps my face in his gloved hands and presses his lips to mine. The kiss leaves me breathless. "You're *shy,*" he murmurs against my lips. "I *like* that..."

I don't want to touch him; I want to kill him for all that he's done to my Tim, but I know that I must keep him occupied momentarily for the sake of the safety of my friends.

"Yes," I say, as he removes my robe and grasps me in his gloved hand. I gasp, and he kisses my shoulder.

"Stop *trembling*, Boy, I'm not going to hurt you..." He again puts his lips to mine, but softly and tenderly this time.

My heart is pounding, and my body is beginning to respond to his. Hating myself, I press him close, and tangle my fingers in his long, blond hair. It falls to the middle of his back, and although the color isn't as striking as Arik's, it's very beautiful indeed. We end up making passionate love, and when Obadiah finally sleeps, I study him momentarily, trying to plot my next move, and then I take my leave.

~*~*~*~

After a hot bath, I dress once more in a clean pair of faded blue jeans and a white oxford shirt, borrowed from Yoshiki, and I go down the hall to check on Benediction. He's sitting up in bed, Ville, as always, at his side.

"Benediction, how *are* you, Man?"

He smiles wearily. "Matthias...you're up awfully late."

"How are you feeling?" I ask him, and I touch his cheek with the back of my hand. "Beni', you're still burning up."

He grins. "So does that make me the hottest guy in the room?"

Ville and I look at each other and laugh.

"Oh, *Beni',*" I groan. "That's corny."

"I'm feeling better, My Dear," he smiles, and his smile grows wider as he sees Brian and Jesse enter the room.

"Hi, Beni'," Brian smiles shyly, and Beni' opens his arms.

"Come to me, My Children..."

"'Morning, Dad," Jesse smiles to him, and Benediction's face lights up with a radiant glow.

"Jesse, My Son, I love you *so!"*

Jesse rushes to him and throws his arms around him.

"How are you?" Jesse asks, hugging him.

"I'm better *now,"* Benediction smiles at him lovingly, tears in his beautiful eyes as he strokes Jesse's hair. Jesse kisses his cheek, and Beni' kisses his, then he hugs Brian with the other arm. "Precious Darling, how *are* you?" he smiles, and Brian blushes.

"Fine," he says bashfully.

"Good," he grins, and catches my eye. I know that I must be smiling like an idiot right now, but I don't care. Benediction knows me, though. He can read my heart. He reaches into my mind and speaks silently to me.

'Where is Timothy?'

'He's not well, Beni'. Obadiah beat the hell out of him.'

'WHAT? OBADIAH??? How in the world--'

'He's one of Hana's clients, I don't know how. I slept with him...I was afraid that he'd find Tim--'

'Where is Tim now?'

'With Arik, in the bedroom.'

'Make sure they stay there--'

'Beni'--'

'Buh! DO AS I SAY!!!'

"All right," I tell him, aloud, and I go back to the bedroom. Tim and Arik are not there, but Hana-No-Seishin is in the hallway. I quickly go to him.

"Hana, what is Obadiah doing here?"

"He is a loyal customer," Hana tells me with annoyance.

"He *kills* people, Hana!!!"

"We have an arrangement," Hana frowns.

"What kind of arrangement?" I cry. "How can you *trust* him?"

"He is *just*, in his way," Hana explains. "He helps us out, and we keep this a secret from the church. We are born what we are. Obadiah is a man who enjoys the company of other men. The church wouldn't understand. You're all safe here."

"He hurt my *Tim,*" I say, my voice husky with tears. "He's bruised up pretty badly. You call that *safe???*"

"I will *wager* that it's not the *first* time that this has happened to him," Hana says rather shortly. I am thunderstruck.

"Well, *no*, but--"

"You are very *new* to this, I can tell," Hana tells me. "This is all part of the job. You will get *used* to it. I'm sure that Timothy understands--"

I can take no more. I slap his face, then turn on my heel and march back to the bedroom, where Tim and Arik have reappeared. They are both freshly dressed, and Arik is applying heavy makeup to the bruises on Tim's beautiful face.

"Matty!" Tim smiles, and I feel a tug in my heart. He sounds tired, but he looks much better. Arik and I glance at each other. Arik's face is very grim, but his eyes are glimmering like prisms. Timothy is his heart as well, although he is keeping it together much more than I. Very gently, I take Tim's slender hand in mine and kiss it.

"Tim, you don't have to *do* this," I tell him, and he plucks his hand out of mine very abruptly and looks very sour.

"And *what* do you expect me to do for money? Paint houses? Shoe horses? *Hmmmm???"* He's tapping his boot at me, and I grit my teeth. He knows that I *hate* it when he does that. Shit, he is *furious.* I know that I'm going to get it now. Both of his hands are on his hips, his eyes are fiery, and burning into mine...hell, I've never been more turned on in my entire life. As I contemplate the least dangerous pathway back to Tim's good graces without getting his boot in my ass, there is a sudden loud cry from Benediction behind my psychic wall.

'MATTY!!!' He's calling me, *'MATTY, come quickly now!!!'*

I turn from Tim and Arik and race to Benediction's bedroom, and what I find there is my worst fear realized...

~*~*~*~

Obadiah is standing just inside the doorway, bloody, dripping sword in hand. He does not notice me behind him as he strides towards Benediction's bed. Jesse steps in front of him, and Obadiah hesitates. Jesse has always been rather a pet of his, and Jesse is the Son of his God...but his righteous anger is overtaking his love and reverence for Jess at an alarming rate.

"What's the trouble, Jesse? Are you *insane*, Boy? You know not whom you protect!!!"

"I *know,*" Jesse says evenly. "This man is my father."

"You ought to be *ashamed,*" he snarls at Jesse, and violently pushes him aside. He points the sword at Benediction's throat. "I want to hear you plead for your life, *Oh Defiler of Humanity*--"

"How *odd* of you to call me that," Benediction states with wonder "When the one that you follow has slaughtered *billions*...and yet, not one war has ever been fought in *my* name."

"Shut *up!"* Obadiah shouts, and the tip of the blade pierces the hollow at the base of Beni's throat. Beni' grunts, and the blood flows down his chest, staining the bandages. I start forward, but Beni' stops me silently, with a look.

[77]

"Jesse, *do* something," I plead, and Jesse, once again, drapes himself protectively over Benediction.

"The blood on your sword," I say to Obadiah, my voice dangerously low, teeth clenched. "I saw it when I walked in. Whose *is* it???"

Obadiah sneers.

"The boy's. The beautiful one, *there.*" He gestures to the left of him, and it's only then that I notice Brian in the chair, bent over at an odd angle.

"Oh, no no no..." I cry, rushing to Brian's side. He is still conscious, but barely. The sword has cut deeply across his shoulder and arm. I pull off my shirt and bind the wound, trying in vain to stop the flow of blood. I weep.

Benediction does as well.

"He is an *innocent!*" Beni' cries.

"He was in the way," Obadiah says absently, and turns back to Jesse, who throws his arms wide in a protective gesture and shields Beni'.

"You *MONSTER!!!!!*"

We all turn with a start to the doorway, where Tim and Arik are standing. Arik looks frightened, but Tim is shaking with fury.

He is magnificent.

"Get *away* from him, you fucking piece of trash!!!!"

"Tim, *no,*" Arik pleads, but Tim pulls away from him, and stalks over to Obadiah, eyes blazing.

Obadiah's eyes are wide, and all the color has drained from his face.

"TIMOTHY!" he gasps, and the sword falls from his hand as he backs away in terror. "H-h-how--???"

Tim keeps advancing on him, and he bares his teeth. The feral glow alights in his eyes, and his fangs cut through.

"You will *never* kill again," Tim tells him, as he takes the fallen sword into his hand. Obadiah's back meets the wall, and he cowers away from Timothy. "*How* did you know that Beni' was here??? *HUH????*" He snarls, and Obadiah turns his head away.

"T-th-the Lord spoke to my heart," he stammers, cowering, as Tim points the sword at Obadiah's throat.

"Jesse, is this *true?*" I ask, and Arik glares at him as well.

"*Is* it--???"

"No, no, My Children," Benediction says solemnly. "Obadiah lies, even now. He came to this place for pleasure, nothing more. He saw me as he passed by the bedroom this morning. Jesse is innocent."

I am startled as the scent of jasmine nearly overpowers me. Arik is frozen in terror, and he is staring at Tim and Obadiah.

"Tim," he pleads, as Tim lays the blade of the sword against Obadiah's throat and bares his teeth at him. "Oh, Timmy, *don't!*"

Tim presses the blade deeper, and a thin line of scarlet appears.

Obadiah closes his eyes, and begins to whisper a silent prayer.

Tim's eyes have the full feral glow. They have the moon in them. The sight of the blood has awakened his hunger.

I take Arik by the arm and pull him back into the corner with Brian.

"He is *yours*, Timothy," Benediction states very seriously. "Do what you will."

Tim hesitates, studying Obadiah with his eyes, the eyes as green and merciless as the stained glass of a cathedral window. Obadiah shudders. All of the years of pain, emotional hurt, and extreme terror exit Timothy in a blood-curdling scream, and the immortal blood beats within him full force.

"You will *die,*" Timothy snarls. "I will show you the mercy that you showed Noah...you will suffer as you deserve to, as you've made *me* suffer--"

Benediction closes his eyes and bows his head. He looks so sad. Ville takes his hand and squeezes it.

"Don't look," I tell Arik, who presses his face to my chest. "It will be over soon, Baby."

"Timothy," Obadiah gasps, as Tim's lips follow the blade in its slow, deadly journey across his throat. "Tim, I-I *loved* you--" He gags, and it is all over for him. Tim feeds ravenously, the blood arcing out to drench him in scarlet. He is crying, he is laughing, he is singing, as only those who have been liberated can. He catches my eye; we smile at one another...

~*~*~*~

...And tonight, we find ourselves at the church once more. We carry a figure shrouded in white between us. Yes, we are an odd sight. Two angels, two of us in bandages, the rest in our regal, splendid dress.

We have spent the afternoon in discussion, and we all agree that this is indeed the right thing to do. Obadiah will live again, as he was truly meant to live. He will become an immortal, his eternal outrage. We shall guide him in these future days, and nurture him as our Brother. For he is what he is...as all of us only can be to ourselves. He will be able to love again.

He will finally be free.

The End